C000184096

Andrew Watts
newtecnic.com

© 2007 Springer-Verlag/Wien
Printed in England
SpringerWienNewYork is a part of Springer
Science+Business Media
springer.at

Layout and Cover Design: Yasmin Watts
Printing and binding: Latimer Trend & Co Ltd

Printed on acid-free and elemental chlorine-free
bleached paper

SPIN: 12030842

Library of Congress Control Number: 2007929745

With numerous coloured figures

978-3-211-71538-3 SpringerWienNewYork

Edited by Andrew Watts
n e w t e c n i c
facade technology + research

SCRATCHING THE SURFACE

NEW LONDON FACADES BY LONDON ARCHITECTS

contents

4_ projects

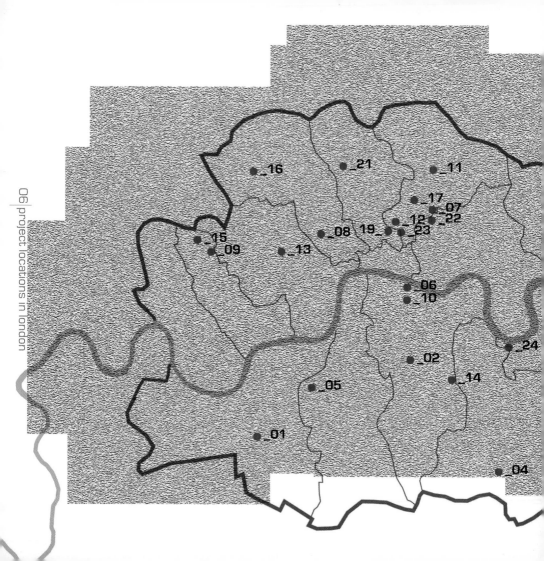

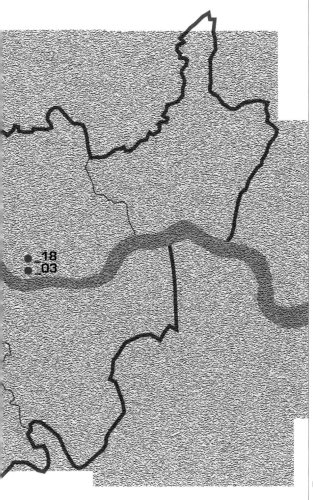

bold red line denotes inner boroughs of london

1 _introduction
essays
interviews
projects

an overview_andrew watts

Scratching the Surface was an exhibition held at the Building Centre Trust in London in the summer of 2007. The exhibition was curated by Newtecnic, facade consultants based in London who work on large-scale ambitious projects around the world. Newtecnic is led by Andrew Watts, who wrote this introduction.

London architecture demonstrates a diverse range of contemporary positions on design; the dialogues between the background and foreground, complex form and rectilinear geometry, sustainability, technological advancement, tradition and change, with each demanding an approach which is more than merely cosmetic. The facade occupies a uniquely complex position as the public face of these new architectural approaches while integrating intelligent systems, environmental, material and structural functions.

Scratching the Surface was an exhibition held at the Building Centre Trust in London in the summer of 2007, and this associated publication explores the current state of the building envelope in London, as proposed by London-based architects. Glimpses into the spectrum of new facades are presented through essays in digital fabrication, material constraints and parametric modelling, all part of the search for a contemporary interpretation of the London vernacular.

A map on the following pages shows the geographical spread of locations of projects in the inner London region. While a cluster are set in Hackney, there is a wide spread across the capital, reflecting the current buoyancy of the economy in London. Some projects are unbuilt,

but most are either nearing completion or have been recently finished, allowing the changes made to the fabric of the city to be keenly observed. Most projects are relatively modest in scale, which is to be expected from the group of architects who have designed them, part of the emerging scene of London architecture. The modesty in scale allows each project to be examined in some detail; most can be visited or are visible from the street. Maps showing the location of each project are there to orientate the reader but not all can be visited. Readers are advised to contact the architects to check of their current status and to ascertain whether they can be visited. A few projects are not visible from the street, and for these examples the nearest Underground Station is not listed, as is also the case where the projects have not yet been constructed. Areas of London where some of the projects have not yet been built are still worthy of a visit, particularly in Hoxton and along the Regent's Canal from the Angel to Victoria Park in Hackney, where many other new schemes are under way.

A set of interviews has been included in the book in order for the reader to become better acquainted with the specific approach of some of the architects. We would have liked to have interviewed all the architects who are exhibiting, but time pressures have made that not possible to achieve, so a selection of seven architects was made that attempts to reflect some of the wide range of approaches taken in the design of contemporary buildings in London, while allowing a common thread of the experience of working in London to be woven across all the interviews.

The accompanying set of essays aims to set out some of the issues which are of interest to the scene of emerging architects in London, such as fabrication using digital technology that allows the designer to have ever closer involvement in the evolution of the built form of the project. Linked to this is an interest in architects working with construction materials in different ways, some which are contemporary interpretations of historic techniques, others which are a result of the manufacturing technique employed. An essay on parametric design has been added. While this development of CAD is only just beginning to emerge in architectural practice, projects such as the Temporary Visitors Centre for the Cutty Sark, at Greenwich, are making use of the form finding capabilities of parametric design software. An essay on developments in new facade systems uses, as examples, projects developed in the Cahill/Watts design studio at the University of Bath. Scott Cahill, with whom I run the studio, has contributed two essays

about the use of materials and constraints imposed by their use, a theme which runs through the projects illustrated in the essay on facade systems. Some of the construction techniques and materials used are finding their way into new projects in London, with some tantalising glimpses of these changes being visible in the projects shown here. The example of a possible evolution of concrete as a construction material is shown here in order to demonstrate the increasing complexity of thought in the use of material, a way of thinking about materials, components and assemblies in facades and structures which is as fundamental as the primary decisions made about the overall organisation, layout and design of the building project

In the new London projects illustrated here progressive technologies and contemporary architectural concerns are enabling designers to take ever closer interest in the sensuality of the facades of buildings, generating outer surfaces of both beauty and depth. The tactile and technical presentation of Scratching the Surface goes some way towards demonstrating that while facades have previously appeared dominated by a visual bias, their role is more than just skin deep.

2_ essays

This essay provides an overview of concrete, supporting research which seeks to define opportunities for more complex applications of the material. This research seeks to engage the naturally heterogeneous characteristics of concrete in combination with advanced production strategies.

Production Strategies

The use of building materials in architectural design can be seen as the translation of raw material into what are usually composite products through a significant amount of industrial intervention. Complex properties and behaviours are embodied within any raw material and the degree to which they are engaged by industry or within architecture will either foster or deny an individual's awareness of these conditions. Therefore, within the practice of architecture, the application of a more knowledgeable material strategy that would integrate considerations associated with the production process of a material could contribute to a greater awareness of the higher level of sophistication that exists within the natural environment.

Currently, the development of material systems for buildings are intimately linked to strategies for production in order to formulate efficient solutions to mass market requirements. The economic benefits of efficient production methods are also linked to advantages in the construction or assembly process. As a result, the ideology of efficiency through redundancy has led our profession to accept component driven design solutions to most architectural problems. To its detriment, the need for efficiency when combined with a high concern for redundancy results in an assembly of building components that is simplistic with respect to the scale of its considerations. The outcome is often a building assembly that is a response to a linear isolation of a minimum quantity of variables and results in a product that offers both a predictable and uniform response.

How could the deficiencies inherent within conventional component design be minimised? Limitations such as the linear isolation of variables, uniformity in application, uniformity in performance and the insistence upon redundancy in production need to be countered with less conventional design and manufacturing techniques. The primary objective should be to engage the underlying properties inherent within the material and its form so that variable responses may become correlated with specific and localised applications. In doing so, a more complex built environment would result in which an edifice would be more closely synchronized with both the properties of its physical form and context.

Case Study: Concrete

Let us examine the case of concrete as a building material. As a cast material, concrete is not as elegant

 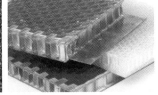 

A foamed material is saturated within ceramic base and mixed. This composite material is oven fired and the foamed material burnt away leaving the ceramic as a porous sponge that is very lightweight and hard.

A sandwich panel typically consists of three layers. Their interdependent relationship provides a material that is resistant to both compression and bending while offering a positive weight/stability ratio.

Elastomers provide a material that is flexible and elastic. Flexibility in form-making allows for the production of a specific formal configuration that is capable of responding to localized and unique stress concentrations.

and efficient as other more advanced materials, but there are still tangible benefits that make its use highly logical. For instance, as a commonly utilized material, its inclusion in the palette of a building ensures that the required learning curve for a conventional labour force when working with the material is minimal. Concrete is also relatively inexpensive, and the plasticity of its application allows for flexibility in manufacturing or constructing a wide range of components, such as columns or floor slabs. In addition, although redundancy and prefabrication could be utilised there would be no need for a manufacturing alliance that woud require a significant capital investment for a single building project.

Through offering specificity in the selection of a material system at a very localized level, a material assembly can be evolved that allows for a more advanced level of efficiency in the process of customizing a component for a particular application. In recent architectural history, discourse has been primarily rooted in ideological debate that uses a method of evaluation or validation within the design process that is an extension of philosophical or often subjective criteria. In contrast with this approach, an alternative means for evolving a design can be used, which correlates external checks or reference information - a process that has more in common with the scientific method of biological or technical studies than the ideological discourse of the social sciences or humanities. This essay offers a description of the methods to be implemented.

In the case of concrete, by controlling heterogeneity within the material composition through the employment of a gradated distribution of aggregate within the component, a material gradient can be achieved through a strategy known as density banding. A controlled variation in aggregate differentials might be used in coordination with a variation in performance criteria within a single concrete component, with each band of aggregate intended to correspond with a particular requirement.

This strategy could be combined with methods for describing the defining features for the component's physical geometry through mathmatical relationships. If certain elements of an object can be reduced to numerical terms alterations to the digital component may be more efficiently transcribed. This would allow for greater ease in the final production of variations

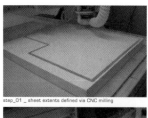
step_01 _ sheet extents defined via CNC milling

step_03 _ assembly of planar sheets into complete formwork

step_05 _ cement/water/sand mixture

step_02 _ three dimensional definition via CNC milling

step_04 _ formwork ready for pouring process

step_06 _ concrete mixture poured within formwork

for a potential component.

An example taken here is a loadbearing structural concrete component which provides, in a single form, a column, external wall, floor slab and an opening for daylight. The diagrams on the following pages highlight a comparison between the method used to produce this component with a more conventional structural envelope in order to highlight efficiencies in the proposed component strategy. In addition, a description of digital modelling processes would be used that coordinate with CNC production techniques in order to produce a formwork construction for the component. The intent is that the component proposal necessitates fewer processing stages and industry associations, while still offering a similar capacity for component customisation.

A New Component Strategy

Concrete was essentially the first heterogeneous man-made building material. In modern applications it is typically composed of steel, sand, gravel and water, and includes cement as the active agent forcing the hardening. However, except for variations in local strengthening where values for compressive and tensile strength may be altered, the material is commonly applied homogeneously as a monolithic or component application within building construction.

In comparison with concrete, however, there is a common tendency in nature that, through the manipulation of the chemical composition and hierarchical arrangement of the same basic molecules, it is possible to extract several different types of material properties. With respect to the heterogeneous nature of concrete, speculation on variable arrangements to suit multiple applications that are beyond the obvious seems to be lacking. As a result, the argument here is to develop a better understanding of the composition matrix of concrete, as well as its strengthening and forming processes in order to speculate on where alterations can be made to both material behaviour and performance criteria. These speculations might allow for more sophisticated applications within a structural assembly or allow for gradient changes of performance to meet local external conditions.

In general, there are two primary mechanisms that lead to failure for all materials, elastic deformation (plastic flow) and brittle cracking. The manner in which a material fails with respect to either of these mechanisms will determine its classification. As a result of the way in which a material is used or structured, the potential for failure is always present. For this reason a brief discussion concerning the acknowledged condition of brittleness within concrete is of value in order to allow for a more accurate understanding of the primary cause for failure.

In contrast to a ductile material, which accepts a great deal of irreversible distortion before fracture due to dislocations within its molecular make-up, a brittle solid allows for only a small amount of elastic strain to take place, primarily at the point of initial loading, before experiencing failure due to cracks that typically run cleanly through the material. The most obvious way of preventing this type of failure is to avoid subjecting the structure to tension, and instead introduce only compressive forces. Unfortunately, a material that is used exclusively in compression has only limited opportunities for fundamental alteration to its composition, namely either variation in compressive strength or material lightness.

As a result of using smaller aggregate in conjunction with a greater quantity of fine aggregate in concrete, the resulting increase in its compressive strength in a structural application results in greater material density. Consequently, the properties of concrete are altered, increasing its impermeability to both audible

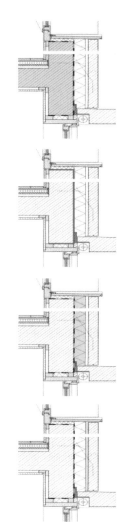

performance constraint 1: structure
Structure is set behind the insulation layer. The aggregate type best suited for this application is one that is both dense and fine. The finer the aggregate, the more compact the mixture composition will be - therefore also providing resistance to crack propagation.

performance constraint 2: waterproof membrane
This membrane prevents the transfer of condensate through the structural layer of the section. A very dense concrete using a well compacted mix of fines aggregate is capable of avoiding the presence of this porous microstructure and avoiding the absorption of water.

performance constraint 3: thermal insulation
This material minimises heat loss/gain by slowing the conduction of heat. It also protects the structure from temperature fluctuations. The most effective insulation is air, as it is more resistant to conduction than a solid material. Consequently, a porous concrete section provides a higher insulation value than a dense section.

performance constraint 4: air cavity
An air space provides a continuous air flow to dry out any condensate that has managed to penetrate the rainscreen. The airspace requires vertical continuity to allow for gravity to direct the condensate to the base of the section.

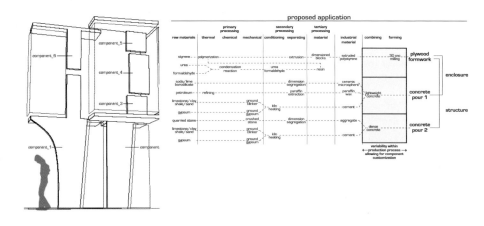

proposed application

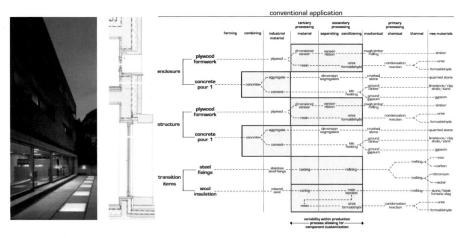

conventional application

sound and water penetration. As moisture absorption decreases, this reduces the need for concrete coatings or protection to any embedded steel reinforcement, as steel will be less prone to rust, which is a condition that typically results in internal fracture of the concrete. The thickness of concrete cover with respect to the steel may also be reduced, resulting in material savings. Although they are more more expensive (perhaps a 50%-200% premium), high strength concretes allow for thinner cross sections within the structure which translates into cost saving on a cubic metre basis of the material. In addition to specifically high strength concretes, self compacting, or reactive powder concretes (which use an even higher percentage of fines and allow for even greater strength) provide savings in the process of application and subsequent treatment of defects. With high strength and high density concrete, many performance related issues of enclosure are addressed within the one layer of concrete, making multi-layered wall assemblies unnecessary.

In contrast to a material with greater density, variations within the concrete mix also allow a lighter weight use of the material while maintaining sufficient compressive strength, though much reduced. This use of concrete is normally achieved by aggregate substitutions, where either a lighter weight filler such as burned clay pellets or polystyrene beads is substituted for the stone aggregate, or an active foaming agent is placed into the mix in order to create enclosed air pockets within the final hardened structure. Due to a less dense material composition the implementation of this technique could result in a high thermal insulation value and is well suited to an external application, therefore avoiding the need for supplementary thermal insulation at floors and walls.

In a similar manner, and in contrast with concrete of a higher material density (where sound transmission is reduced through the deflection of sound waves), lightweight concrete has a high capacity for sound absorption. This quality of absorption by its porous structure results in a material with a slightly greater water retention rate and therefore requires protective coatings or membrane barriers. In common with lightweight materials, concrete of this design has the added benefit of requiring fewer material resources and therefore allows for a lighter structure leading to lower energy expenditure in the forming process. As opposed to the more dense composition of concrete, the more porous nature of this mix requires the use of a multi-layered wall construction when used as an external wall.

In general, these two variations are worth noting relative to brittleness as the thinner and lighter a concrete structure becomes, the more prone it is to failure through cracking due to lack of toughness as bending and tensile loads become more prominent. Designing concrete to embody an increase in toughness requires an increase in the work of fracture within its material or molecular composition, possibly via the inclusion of dislocations or seams that enable crack stopping. To seek natural systems for influence, natural non-metallic materials that exhibit toughness often contain interfaces or planes of weakness within materials, and are commonly heterogeneous as they consist of two or more constituents.

A solid material is often classified according to its tensile and compressive strength, values which across the spectrum of materials exist entirely independent of one another. The strength of a material corresponds to the amount of force needed to break it, physically pulling the atoms apart that chemically bind

Detail view of dense composition of high strength concrete.

Aerated concrete is achieved by mixing a concentrated foaming chemical with water and compressed air and generating foam. The foam is poured into the concrete mixer and mixes it with the sand/cement/water slurry. Weight reductions from 10% to 87% will result depending on mix proportions and materials.

its molecular arrangement. As previously explained, due to its classification as brittle material (lacking toughness), concrete is best used in compression. Upon introducing loading conditions that result in bending or tensile forces, concrete exhibits a lack of strength, resulting in cracking and eventually failure of the material. This implies that the chemical bonds of its molecular arrangement are relatively easy to pull apart, particularly at the junction of differing materials. As a result of this condition, it is clear that in order to strengthen concrete, methods must be used to decrease the magnitude of brittleness, as the two qualities are fundamentally linked. In other words, in order to allow concrete to exhibit greater strength under tensile load, one must devise mechanisms that inhibit the molecular bonds from pulling cleanly apart.

An effective strategy for the reduction of crack ex-

pansion requires knowledge of the internal surfaces of materials within the composite mix. Within nature it is common to see interfaces between contrasting materials that are generally weaker than the materials themselves. This is not a result of nature exhibiting an inability to glue the surfaces together properly, but instead because weak interfaces contribute to the strengthening of a material by making it tough. For example, trees are able to resist the extreme bending that results from high wind forces as a result of the thin outer layer of bark being set in tension, which resists strain imposed by bending action. Although the inner fibrous structure may resist tensile forces, due to the natural prestressing which exist in most fibrous structures, its primary load bearing capacity is directed towards to transferring the compressive load of the tree into the ground. A similar technique for strengthening is used in annealed glass, although

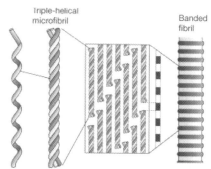

Three dimensional weaving and thin wire reinforcement.

Collagen is a protein based structural material composed of chain molecules that gather together in complex arrangements to form hierarchical arrangements of ropes woven from string that is woven from thread. Collagen aggregates in various ways to form microfibrils which may then combine again to form fibrils.

with the location of tensile and compressive elements reversed, a logic that is perhaps capable of transferring to concrete structures.

The conventional strategy for separating compressive and tensile forces within the material would allow the inclusion of thin fibre and microscopic weaving patterns to provide greater flexibility in the design of form. Strength would be increased for reasons similar to those discussed previously, assuming that weaves and fibres are long in length (short fibres do not require enough of a detour for the travel of cracks and are therefore ineffective). Fibres are essentially three dimensional weaves but, like collagen, a greater strength is derived than if they were placed independently due to their hierarchical arrangement of threading. In both fibres and weaves, a direction of strength must usually be biased as they are both vector based,

resulting in an anisotropic composite material. Also, the use of technical textiles made of glass or carbon means that concrete cover can be reduced as rusting of steel is no longer an issue, therefore allowing for thin walled, three dimensionally shaped elements that may offer a more natural response to internal force requirements. As innovations develop in concrete design, cross sections will continue to get smaller and the fibre will possibly even become the dominant material, leading to what is often otherwise referred to as a bonded fibre material, and thus contribute to a much reduced use of raw materials for a particular structure.

Typically within the construction industry, the shape of a structural assembly and the methods of construction are dictated by social and economic biases which ensure efficiency within the building process. As a

A bone network seeks an efficient response to it's continually evolving loading requirements. Instead of making significant alterations to its form, a bone adjusts the distribution of its cellular material to provide regions of greater physical density where areas of stress are higher due to force translation. These localized areas can vary throughout the bone in direct response to the stress gradient.

A leaf stem is a cantilevered load and seeks an effective method for the translation of this load to the branch of the tree. The simplest and most effective means to achieve this is to alter a portion of the cross section (at the stem) and to provide a build-up of cellular material that is capable of resisting the compressive load produced at the leaf cantilever. The section can vary throughout the length of the leaf in response to the load requirement.

In addition to the compressive force produced by the dead load of the tree (a stress that is most effectively addressed through the form and molecular build-up of the tree trunk), wind loads introduce lateral stress. In response the cross section of the tree has evolved a differentiated material system within which an external layer of bark is located at the surface where it is positioned to most effectively respond to the tensile stresses that arise at the windward face.

Within the molecular organization of all materials natural seams exist between grouped molecules which may combine in any number of ways to impart different effects upon similar materials. Within a brittle material these natural seams are more pronounced and do not possess the capacity for absorbing energy induced from an applied stress - therefore enabling crack propagation to occur. In order to increase toughness (combat brittleness) many natural materials have evolved means for more densely packing material matter, thereby making seams either less pronounced or less direct - and therefore increasing the materials capacity for absorbing energy.

result, within most forms of construction the magnitude of the internal stress within a structure is the result of the shape acting in response to specific loading conditions, and quite often this correlation is arbitrary. Biological processes within nature take an alternative approach. In nature the operation and evolution of form demonstrates that a principle exists which demands efficiency in energy use in combination with a sparing use of natural resources (image 2.8) - in other words, within nature shape is cheaper than material. A similar strategy for the efficient use of materials within the built world is slowly evolving due to an emerging interest in minimum or lightweight structures. Often within this approach, and in correlation with biological concerns where conservation of energy and material is prioritised, a designer is likely to be concerned with how much strength or stiffness is achieved for a given weight.

These concerns are interesting to consider relative to the forming process of concrete, as its plastic nature allows for local variation in form that may respond to, instead of dictating, internal stresses brought about by external loading requirements. This condition theoretically allows for efficiency in material use and therefore weight, and is only limited by what is financially viable. It seems that as concrete mixes develop, greater strength in combination with decreased thicknesses, and therefore more easily formed profiles, and there should be the opportunity to introduce flexible forming processes that would remove the requirement for material redundancy and allow for an 'ideal' distribution of forces within a structure, the ideal corresponding to a constant array of internal forces where stress would be equally distributed between every point of the structure and in every direction, thus avoiding shear forces.

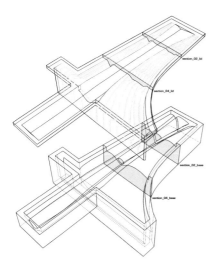

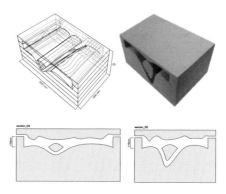

Although flexibility in form making has obviously been limited by economic constraints do to the redundancy of craftsmanship involved, there is potential for CNC (computer numerical control) milling to offer the required efficiency through the removal of redundant labour, as a CNC machine can perform variations as easily as a repeating one endlessly. In the case of concrete form work this may be done through subtractive fabrication, which involves the removal of a specified volume of material from a solid via multi axis milling. An additional strategy that allows for the formation of force responsive concrete structures uses pneumatic form work. Within this process an air filled structure is employed on site and sprayed from the inside with an insulating layer. To this layer reinforcement is applied (from the inside), and then concrete is sprayed over this to provide coverage. Upon hardening, the air filled structure on the exterior can be removed and

the top insulating layer coated to meet user requirements. Openings within the structure for windows and entry are blocked off from spraying at the beginning of the process. This technique in its current form is limited as the concrete can only be applied through a spraying process, as any other method would disturb the pneumatic form work, and this implies that the structure relies on secondary applications for smooth finishing.

The component proposal outlined within this essay represents a material strategy for effectively providing localized variation in performance capacities for an individual component that could be capable of responding to site specific requirements. In addition, a corresponding production strategy is identified which enables for variability to be accomodated within the components form.

It has been proposed within the hypothesis of the previous essay that considerations of material properties, performance criteria and formal configurations are best considered as interdependent in order to develop a more effective component application. A comprehensive approach such as this is intended to allow for a more efficient use of material as it will not be conventionally applied to address generic and global application criteria, but instead more effectively related to variable and local concerns This essay documents a specific example in which a comprehensive understanding of material and performance related strategies define opportunities and limitations inherent within the formal configuration of the component design.

In correlation with the development of formal strategies, rules dictating the components geometric definition will be extrapolated in order to enable control over discrete characteristics of the component with greater specificity. Such a strategy will provide a time efficient method for evolving alterations to the component's localized formal properties - and in doing so allow for an efficient method of propagating alternative solutions to specific constraints. This technique, when correlated with an appropriate method of analysis, is intended to operate in the interest of developing a more optimized component application.

Firstly, however, it will be beneficial to review general classifications concerning prefabricated construction techniques in order to provide a reference resource for any component strategy devised within this essay. Although the benefits of these strategies are obvious, general specificities of their attributes are highlighted below for review:

_ Repetition within a predetermined design strategy will result in a shorter period for design development (A realistic time period might be as little as four weeks, however, Toyota homes and Ikea have reduced this period to two hours).

_ Controlled factory conditions mitigate concerns for weather variability and therefore allow for a more efficient production of specific components.

_ Off-site prefabrication requires fewer trades on site, allowing for a more ordered and efficient site and contributing to fewer defects in the finishing of the building.

modular technologies

This strategy incorporates a redundancy of components that allow for ease of design, interchangeability and assembly. Potentially 80 to 90 percent of the construction may be done in a factory, limiting on-site work to the foundation, septic system and some finishes. The most conventional techniques employ wood framed sections 14-16 feet wide.

panelised/kit construction

A strategy popularized by the Sears, Roebuck Company in 1908 through their do-it-yourself house kits. The design of the house may be ordered and then customised to suit client design specifications. The components are then pre-cut and pre-manufactured and shipped to the site with instructions for assembly.

manufactured design

Often a reference to a housing unit completely assembled within controlled factory conditions and then shipped to site for installation, formerly a category applicable to North American mobile homes, although this is now classified as a less stringent form of construction. A permanent chassis is required to assure transportability.

_ Once on site, the efficient assembly of components allows for the more efficient formation of a building enclosure, and therefore a more efficient completion of the interior finishes.

A description of the proposed component fabrication strategy for the concrete component is outlined below:

_ The components are intended to be pre-cast and produced off site under controlled environmental conditions. The formwork will be made from polystyrene that will be moulded using a CNC milling process, ideally utilizing a five-axis router. Each formwork is anticipated to be used twice per project and will be recycled upon completion.

_ The maximum component dimensions are to be 4.2m x 2m wide so that transport can be undertaken efficiently and erection by a medium size crane is made feasible. It is intended that pre-cast floor planks will be linked with the concrete component enclosure, allowing for overall stability within the entire structure.

_ An external glazing system is to be integrated flush with the edge of the concrete component in order to complete the enclosure. These two systems will ideally be evaluated simultaneously with respect to pre-defined site specific performance related criteria - namely insulation value and the potential for solar gain.

component heterogeneity

Taking concrete as an example, and as discussed in the previous essay, a design strategy for an individual building component will be most effective if formal configurations are correlated with both material properties and performance criteria in an interdependent manner. The research diagram on the following page documents potential instances where this correlation is achievable. As an example, the matrix suggests that a performance requirement such as structural force resolution can be correlated, though not exclusively, with alternative concerns such as material density of the aggregate and the volume of the structural core.

In order for this generative correlation of conventionally distinct data types to operate successfully,

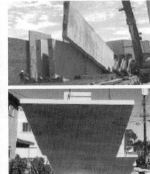

however, a method of directly relating properties must be devised. Such a task can be accomplished via computer scripting techniques which incorporate parametric data, as this demands that distinct and typically physical characteristics are translated into numerical values - allowing for a strategy that facilitates a cross fertilisation of data between separate spheres. The numerical representations then have direct influence upon formal characteristics of the building component.

In addition, as indicated in component diagram it is not possible to solve only for a specific performance condition in isolation, as performance considerations are not only linked with material and formal concerns, but are also linked within themselves. For example, a potential re-configuration within the volume of a structural core containing a certain material density will alter the overall insulation value of the component at this location, therefore dictating changes to the planar section in order to maintain a constant value, and vice versa. Such constraints may be established by either user requirements or site conditions which

therefore implies that this process embodies simplistic top-down/bottom-up processing mechanisms.

Also as discussed in the first essay, current component proposals and material applications within the built environment favour homogeneity and simplicity within material systems as such standards enable predictability. This approach is the result of a predisposition towards linear thinking with respect to problem solving, in which a variable is isolated in order to be resolved, described as a 'reductionist' approach. However, a more heterogeneous material application that is capable of quantifying multiple parameters in parallel is possible, resulting in a more effective application of the material.

A material strategy can be adopted that is capable of integrating multiple performance and programmatic requirements within a single material system. A physical modelling study is outlined which attempts to coordinate component related performance requirements with repeatable self-organising properties of differentiated aggregate systems within an individual concrete

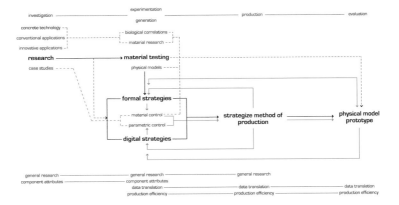

application. This physical model strategy is explored with respect to four variables (water content, cement content, aggregate mix and vibration time) and the variables are only marginally adjusted between tests in order to develop an effective composite mixture.

In nature, a network in a skeletal bone seeks an efficient response to its continually evolving loading requirements. Instead of making significant alterations to it's form, a bone adjusts the distribution of its cellular material to provide regions of greater physical density where areas of stress are higher due to force translation. These localised areas can vary throughout the bone in direct response to the stress gradient.

A leaf stem is a cantilevered load and seeks an effective method for the translation of this load to the branch of the tree. The simplest and most effective means to achieve this is to alter a portion of the cross section at the stem and to provide a build-up of cellular material that is capable of resisting the compressive load produced at the leaf cantilever. The section can vary throughout the length of the leaf in response to the load requirement.

In addition to the compressive force produced by the dead load of the tree (a stress that is most effectively addressed through the form and molecular build-up of the tree trunk), wind loads introduce lateral bending which produce tensile stress. In response the cross section of the tree has evolved a differentiated material system within which an external layer of bark is located at the surface where it is positioned to most effectively respond to the tensile stresses that arise at the windward face.

Within the molecular organization of all materials natural seams exist between grouped molecules which may combine in any number of ways to impart different effects upon similar materials. Within a brittle material these natural seams are more pronounced and do not possess the capacity for absorbing energy induced from an applied stress, therefore enabling crack propagation to occur. sIn order to increase toughness (combat brittleness) many natural mate-

variability in component systems

rials have evolved means for more densely packing material matter, thereby making seams either less pronounced or less direct, increasing the materials capacity for absorbing energy.

It has been suggested in this essay that conventional strategies for mass customisation embody limitations with respect to their ability to derive unique solutions in support of external preferences. The dominant strategy for any product which claims to provide component variability in response to user or environmental requirements, such as a computer, car or home, is for the global product type to allow for the interchanging of slightly variable, but pre-determined and unchanging components. This approach still fundamentally relies upon the expectation that the conventional operations associated with mass production will be employed within the development of individual components. Its promise of accommodating variability is tied to the assumption that the final product will have a broad market demand and one could therefore be able to economically provide a limited number of simplistic variations between components that sug-

gest the capability to respond to user or environmental needs.

In contrast, the component proposal outlined within this dissertation has sought to strategise an efficient means for providing specific and localised geometric and material variation within an individual component, as well as other components within a complete assembly, in order to facilitate the provision of a uniquely customised product. It is significant to note that in tandem with this objective the production strategy that is employed suggests a true release from a reliance upon the operations associated with mass production, including the tendency to engage in speculative production in order to surpass thresholds that allow for a reduction in unit costs, a strategy which instead often leads to the over production of goods and an inefficient use of material on the macro level. However, such an approach is only effective if it is able to successfully shift the emphasis of production efficiency from the realm of industrial production to the designer's digital arena. Most of the techniques documented here aim to facilitate this shift and offer

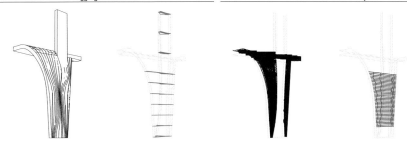

a strong foundation for so doing.

If such a shift can occur within contemporary material assemblies it would imply that society could move away from a material reality that is generic, universal and linear towards one that is local, responsive and multi-parametric. The benefits of this alteration would not only be practical, but conceptual, as it may begin to imply that our constructed world should not be perceived as something that exists in opposition to the natural world. Instead the built world would act in synthesis with natural world. Such a development would contribute to the emerging world view which understands the natural world to be composed of processes as opposed to objects, a logical and positive contribution in the further development of both our social awareness and our understanding of our natural world.

general mix variables

variable 1 _ water content

variable 2 _ cement content

variable 3 _ vibration time

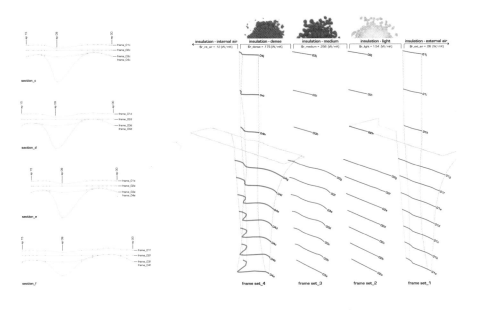

section_c

section_d

section_e

section_f

insulation - internal air
λr_int_air = 12 [W/mK]

insulation - dense
λr_dense = 175 [W/mK]

insulation - medium
λr_medium = 258 [W/mK]

insulation - light
λr_light = 1.54 [W/mK]

insulation - external air
λr_ext_air = 06 [W/mK]

frame set_4

frame set_3

frame set_2

frame set_1

aggregate variables

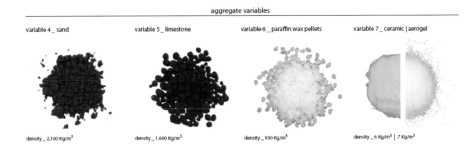

variable 4 _ sand

density _ 2,100 Kg/m³

variable 5 _ limestone

density _ 1,600 Kg/m³

variable 6 _ paraffin wax pellets

density _ 930 Kg/m³

variable 7 _ ceramic | aerogel

density _ 6 Kg/m³ | .7 Kg/m³

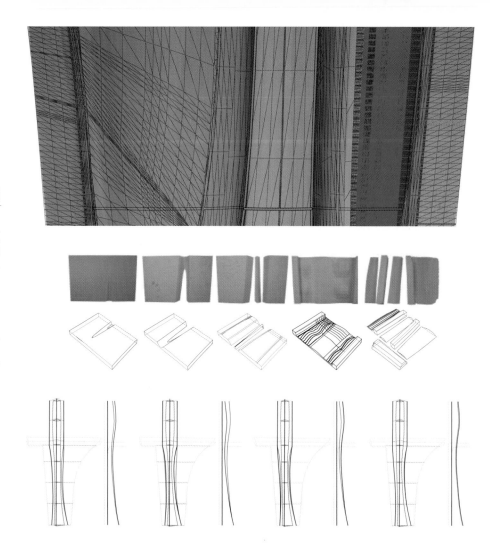

upper plane volume

.00175 m³ = 1750.0 ml

mix ratio	1 : 1 : 4
cement	291.6 ml
water	291.6 ml
ceramic/aerogel	1166.0 ml

mid plane volume

.00612 m³ = 6125.0 ml

mix ratio	1 : .75 : 3
cement	1289.5 ml
water	967.0 ml
ceramic/aerogel	3868.5 ml

upper plane volume

.00490 m³ = 4900.0 ml

mix ratio	1 : .75 : 3
cement	1031.5 ml
water	773.6 ml
ceramic/aerogel	3094.5 ml

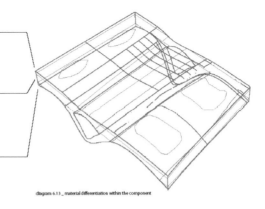

diagram 6.13 _ material differentiation within the component

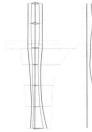
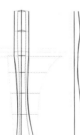

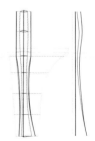

introduction
2 _essays
interviews
projects

The design of facades is being informed increasingly by a greater mastery of the primary materials from which they are constructed. Emerging methods and materials used for thermal insulation allow the primary material to become visible once again, and not be concealed by a 'duvet' in another material.

Recent trends in facade design have developed around the use of singular materials: aluminium, steel, concrete, fabrics and timber. With the introduction of digital technologies for both design and fabrication, and the accompanying link between them in CAD/CAM, there are greater possibilities for more complex components, assemblies and building forms. While complexity in itself is not necessarily a useful quality, the greater interdependence of components in a building, with a multi-functioning role assigned to building assemblies ensures that building structures and envelopes are working ever harder with less material used.

Semi monocoque structures are slowly finding use in building construction, with the control of 3D curved surfaces in CAD packages where surfaces that are curved or twisted can be flattened or 'developed' in or-

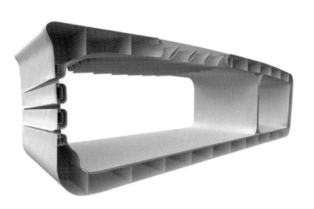

der to provide cutting patterns for manufacture. The ability of a designer to describe a building structure, or building envelope, as a set of fully drawn components, ready for manufacture, is a return to an earlier era of architectural practice, and is very much a return to the craft based work of the designer. Even when every component is drawn, however, the close involvement of the fabricator, manufacturer or installer is critical to the development of these drawings to suit the re-quirements of their equipment or method of working. The precision of both drawing and manufacture is reflected in the ability of semi monocoque structures to avoid the need for a loose fit decorative interior. Both inner and outer skins can be described precisely, avoiding the need for a secondary interior structure sitting within the primary structure. Designers are grasping a closer understanding of how curved panels can be fitted together to avoid awkward junctions or a

Semi monococoque structure by Steve Mason, Cahill/Watts Studio, University of Bath

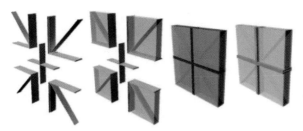

This page:
Loadbearing metal wall structure by Adam Willetts
Next page top:
Semi monococoque structure by John Tredinnick
Next page bottom:
Aerated concrete structure by Barry Stirland
Cahill/Watts Studio, University of Bath

clumsy geometry that gives uneven reflections. May of these lessons are being learned from the automotive industry, where optimising the form finding of curved panels has long been established.

Until recently, a difficulty inherent in metal building envelopes has been one of thermal bridging. The introduction of vacuum insulation panels provides much lower thermal conductivities than those typi-

cally achieved with other thermal insulation materials. Theses materials are made from glass fibre or open cell polymers wrapped in an impermeable film, with manufacturers claiming thermal conductivities up to one tenth that of conventional insulation materials.

Another development in metal envelopes is the load-bearing metal panel with translucent skins on either side. These comprise an aluminium edge frame with

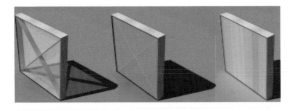

cross bracing, measuring around 500mm square. Translucent panels are filled with a translucent insulation and faced with a polymer based material such as GRP. Opaque panels are metal faced and are filled with a regular thermal insulation material. Thermal breaks across the panel ensure tat condensation is avoided on the inside face of the panel. Although in a development phase, these panels are set to come into use on smaller scale projects.

A recent development in concrete has been the introduction of insulating aggregates, or air bubbles introduced into the concrete mix, which provides much lower U-values. So called 'expanded' concrete has air bubbles that occupy from 30% to 80% of the volume of the mix. This concrete comprises fine aggregates mixed with cement and is foamed mechanically, providing materials of densities between 400kg/m3 and 1600kg/m3. Even the heavier mixes are still consid-

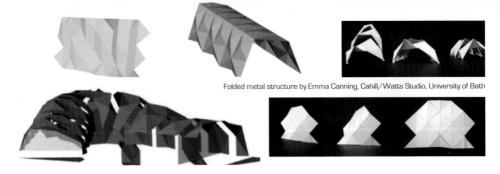

Folded metal structure by Emma Canning, Cahill/Watts Studio, University of Bath

erably lighter than an equivalent lightweight concrete that employs a regular mix. Reasonable strengths can be achieved with expanded concrete mixes. Water absorption is low, but vapour permeability is high, resulting in a need for vapour barriers where appropriate for the application and geographical location.

The flexible nature of fabrics is being used in facades to create elements that move to provide solar shading. Fabrics used are either polymer based, such as PVC coated polyester fabric or PTFE coated glass fibre fabric, or alternatively, woven metal fabrics,

mainly those whose original function was as conveyor belt mesh. The introduction of flexible sheet materials a solar shading, with their ability to take up different forms, is set to develop over the coming years. The 'air pillows' formed as ETFE cushions are undergoing development in a multi layered form. Cushions with patterns printed on one or two additional internal layers, to provide solar shading, can be made to move by gently inflating or deflating the ETFE cushions. This has the effect of changing the alignment of the panels which allows the passage of varying amounts of daylight, which may be at different times of day, or

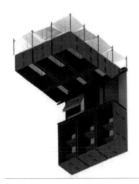
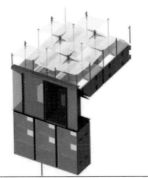

Loadbearing metal structure by Taku Saji, Cahill/Watts Studio, University of Bath

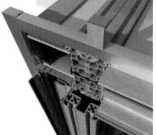

Alumimium and timber structure by Howard Tee, Cahill/Watts Studio, University of Bath

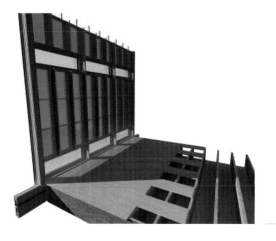

may provide a gradation daylighting at one time. This dynamic facade and roof system can create different daylighting effects, and overcome the difficulty of providing varying levels of sunlight, with its attendant solar gain, at different times of day.

The lightness in weight of ETFE cushions brings also about advantages in a more lightweight supporting system than that required for glass. The support of ETFE cushions has been achieved typically by clamping the perimeter of the panels into extruded aluminium sections that follow a similar principle to glazed curtain walling. Clamps can be fixed back to a more lightweight structure than that required to support glass, with the effect of allowing visually lighter, more refined components to be used, such as nodes which use the rotating connectors to support the structure which are usually used only as connectors for bolt fixed glazing. The use of lightweight timbers is beginning to emerge as an alternative to steel and aluminium

Fabric solar shading by Chris Hill, Cahill/Watts Studio, University of Bath

frames to support ETFE cushion roofs, particularly when used as grid shell structures.

A major development in recent years has been that of the revived use of timber structures, particularly load-bearing walls in solid timber panels. The environmental benefits of timber is well known, but the advantage of monolithic timber panels for walls, floors and roofs are recent, as is the use of CNC cutting machines as a result of being able to provide component draw-ings rather than the standard plans, sections and elevations used in a traditional design approach. With fewer details required to be resolved at junctions, proprietary systems allow designers more freedom to describe all the component parts for walls, floors and roofs. Monolithic timber panels, which are relatively light in weight, have led to an increase in the use of folded plate structures, where panels are triangulated in one form or another, taking their inspiration from the folded paper structures of origami rather than

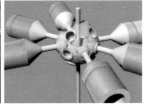

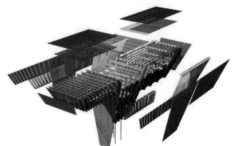

This page: Timber structure by Louise Jarvis
Next page: Timber structure by Rachel Mundell
Cahill/Watts Studio, University of Bath

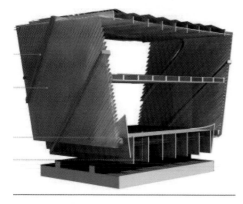

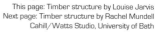

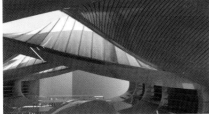

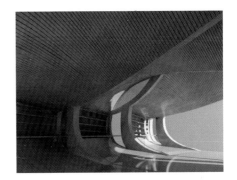

from models of mainstream architecture.

Timber panels are also being used as cladding panels to metal frames, combining the precision of aluminium to form a skeletal frame with the lightweight, low embodied energy of timber. An advantage of timber cladding panels is their inherent flexibility, allowing metal framed windows and translucent panels to be integrated easily as a result of the ease of cutting and joining the material. Loadbearing timber frames are being used for buildings much taller than was traditionally the case. The ability to cut timber digitally has led to the revival of laminated timber structures, providing building envelopes that are much more elegant than equivalent examples of even 10 years ago.

introduction
2 essays
interviews
projects

This essay provides an introduction to digital fabrication. Starting with mass production methods, the tools used in digital fabrication are explained, progressing to examples in North America, where a small group of influential architects are using this approach to inform their design thinking at a fundamental level.

Mass production has had a significant effect on the profession of architecture over the last two centuries. However, it has become clear in recent years that the methods of fabrication it established are being rendered obsolete by the growing sophistication and ubiquity of computer-aided manufacture (CAM).

These new processes have many advantages, but perhaps the most important is the ability to create unique items at a similar speed, quality and cost as identical items made using mass production. By utilizing CAM we can therefore remove the limitations of repetitive building components, and think beyond simplistic formal arrangements. At the same time, however, these technologies also pose new challenges for us by introducing greater complexity into the manufacturing stages of a scheme.

This essay will discuss the full implications of CAM, first by outlining its evolution and the particular characteristics of the different processes within it, then by discussing the work of various architects applying this technology. In order to fully appreciate how significant this change is, we will begin by looking at the origins of mass production and consider the values it impressed upon architecture.

Establishing the Rules – Mass Production

In the early 1800's mechanization had already drastically transformed industry throughout Europe and America. Workshops across the world were producing all manner of machines for the thriving milling, textiles and transport industries. However, the process of manufacturing these pieces of equipment was itself still heavily reliant on the manual skills of machine operators. The US government, in their search for more effective means of producing firearms, poured millions of dollars into research to improve the quality and precision of manufacturing methods. As a result manual operations such as filing were supplanted by broaching and milling, while new advances in drilling and profiling increased efficiency and further emphasized the dominance of machines in the workshop. Within a few years these methods, loosely labelled 'interchangeable manufacturing', had been adopted into other professions and industries, creating the basis for wholesale mass production.

The effects of this change, in combination with the widespread use of division of labour, were numerous. The separation of design and production, begun decades before, was cemented. Workers who had once crafted various materials directly became

Mass production of cars.

Programming a CNC cutting machine.

unskilled machine operators, responsible only for the supervision of a single process or the production of a single part. Likewise their counterparts, the designers, found themselves increasingly isolated from the products of their work.

Prominent figures in architecture such as Walter Gropius and Le Corbusier produced works and theories based on the emerging paradigm of mass production – the latter famously calling for the house to become a "machine for living in"[1]. Although this belief that buildings could be constructed as easily as cars or planes proved premature at the time, it has had a lasting impact on the profession. Such methods of standardization and prefabrication advocated in the 1920's are now common in architecture – playing a major role in the production of cladding systems, windows and many other building elements.

Breaking the Rules – CAM and Mass Customization

Mass production, however, is not as dominant as these examples might suggest. Its position is now threatened by technologies that originally emerged during the 1950s, which married its efficiencies with those of the new discipline of computing.

Initially this new generation of computer-numerically-controlled (CNC) machines differed little from their predecessors. The trained machinist, in one sense replaced by information contained on punched cards and fed into a computer, was still needed for the laborious task of punching the cards. In addition, the accuracy of the resulting work was at times uneven. With the invention of reliable programming languages in the early '60s however, even these slight impositions were removed and the full potential of CNC techniques became apparent.

In the 40 years since then, the range and complexity of operations these CNC machines can undertake has expanded dramatically. Conventional processes like milling and turning have been improved with advances such as 7-axis movement of the drill head, while entirely new processes such as die-less manufacturing offer us innovative methods to mould and form difficult materials. This broad set of procedures are today grouped under the general term Computer-Aided Manufacture (CAM).

Although there are a multitude of different processes, and some are limited to individual companies and manufacturers, Branko Kolarevic has noted that they can be split into just 4 classes – Cutting, Subtractive,

Components CNC milled from polystyrene.

Additive and Formative[2]:

• Cutting Form created by cutting and separating the material from a larger volume. Examples include *plasma-arc, laser-beam* and *water-jet cutting*.

• Subtractive Form created by removing volumes from the material using multi-axis milling. This process can instead be used to produce moulds or formwork that shape the selected material.

• Additive Form created by incrementally depositing and thus building up the material – often applied in layers. Examples include *sprayed concrete forming, stereolithography, fused deposition modelling* and *selective laser sintering* (the final three are all manufacturer's brands for a particular kind of additive CAM process called rapid prototyping). Also known as solid freeform manufacturing or layered manufacturing.

• Formative Form created by applying mechanical forces, restricting forms, heat or steam to the material. Examples include *vacuum forming, numerical bending of rods, tubes or strips of material*, and *die-less manufacturing*.

roof detail from the 2005 Serpentine pavilion by Siza and de Moura.

Clearly all of these techniques have advantages and disadvantages in terms of speed, accuracy, the forms that are achievable, the materials that are suitable, cost, and so on. These characteristics make each process appropriate for certain construction solutions – for example cutting is ideal for the fabrication of designs that are assemblages of planes, by using "sequential sectioning, triangulation...[or] developable surfaces and unfolding"[3]. The 2005 Serpentine pavilion by Siza and de Moura used this process very efficiently – the contractor "never got a proper set of drawings because of the speed of the project – he just got a table of numbers that described the coordinates of every point and the chamfer" needed to cut the 427 unique laminated timber members[4].

Conversely die-less manufacturing can be used to produce true double-curved surfaces (as opposed to simplified developable surfaces) by positioning "arrays of height-adjustable numerically controlled pins" as moulds for different heated materials[5]. This process

MIT's Instant Cabin.

A functional cable tie, with integral hinge, created at Metropolitan Works using rapid prototyping.

makes it possible to directly create complex curved glass forms, and eliminates the time-consuming process of producing intermediate moulds in other materials.

These techniques bring with them other advantages too. Laser cutters, for example, are accurate to within 0.001 inch, which is the tolerance required to make a structure that "fits together without needing fasteners of adhesives"[6]. Members of MIT's Digital Design Fabrication group have invented an entire construction system based on this attribute – creating so-called 'Instant Cabins' that are held together by friction alone and require only a rubber mallet to build[7]. At the same time this method highlights one of CAM's greatest limitations – that the fabrication of large elements often requires that they be broken down into several smaller components (due to the size constraints of the CNC bed they are produced on) and then reassembled. MIT's project has one final benefit – by doing away with glue, screws and nails, their form of press-fit construction also makes disassembly and recycling easier later on.

Similarly certain additive CAM processes can create nested or internally sealed structures that would be impossible to form using any other procedure. For example stereolithography can selectively fix particles of material to create operable moving parts such as hinges or gears[8]. Furthermore, the quality of the resulting pieces is so high that additional finishing is often unnecessary. This fact – combined with other positive characteristics like high strength, good durability and low weight – means these 'prototypes' can be the final product. Matthew Lewis, business development manager of the Metropolitan Works digital manufacturing centre in London, has noted this trend in the work they are commissioned to produce: "more and more the technology is developing into this kind of rapid manufacturing, where the actual parts coming out the machines are the end product, as opposed to the traditional use of the technology which is for prototyping"[9].

These powerful techniques are also complimented by advances in 3D scanning, where hand-held and turntable digitizers trace the key features of an object and produce a point cloud that defines its form. This technology is conventionally used to verify the accuracy of manufactured objects by comparing them with the digital files they are based on. Alternatively, 3D scanning offers a way to record and import the

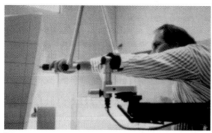
3D scannning is used in the offices of Frank Gehry.

MIT's 3 Dimensional Printing Project can create components in different materials, but with the same fabrication equipment.

complete geometry of physical models into a digital environment, in which they can be further adjusted (a process pioneered in architecture by Frank Gehry).

Following the emergence of all these techniques people began to posit a new branch of manufacturing, called mass customization, in which CAM is used to produce unique, personalized products every time. Indeed one of the overriding advantages of CAM is that "uniqueness is now as economic and easy to achieve as repetition"[10]. While *mass* customization has wider meanings outside the field of architecture, it is a useful label to apply here as it highlights the most fundamental difference between these technologies and their predecessor, mass production.

Future Developments

These examples reveal the flexibility, speed and accuracy that make CAM techniques so advantageous. Unfortunately, they also have one critical constraint in common – they are unable to realise multiple-material designs. Cutting, Subtractive and Formative processes clearly offer no possibility of this, and Additive processes can currently only work with a single material – be it plastic, metal or ceramic.

However, the director of MIT's Centre for Bits and Atoms, Neil Gershenfeld, believes that this problem will be solved within just a few years. He notes that rapid prototyping technology is already being adapted to print from several different material stores, just as colour printers employ different ink cartridges. This improvement could produce more than just straightforward composites as well – Gershenfeld believes it could 'print' circuit boards and therefore electronics: "in the research lab today there are...inks that can be used to print insulators, conductors, and semi-conductors"[11]. Such a situation might seem far fetched, but it is actually highly plausible given that current fabrication technology is analogous with computing hardware 60 years ago. At that time each computer was the size of a room and cost thousands of pounds to purchase and operate, since then computers have obviously shrunk and reduced in price by a huge amount - a process that fabrication equipment has only just begun[12].

Mass Customization in Architecture

Although these technologies are far from perfected, they are already gaining popularity in architecture. A new generation of architects are using these manufacturing techniques to retake control of much

Evans House, by William Massie, utilizes a similar form of construction to his Big Belt House project.

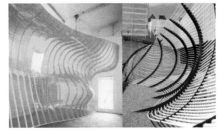

Massie has also applied this form of construction to acrylic and rusted steel, for the WP.S.1 and P.S.1 installations in New York.

of the building process - from design and analysis through to fabrication and construction - which has in turn created opportunities for experimentation rarely seen in the profession.

Massie Architecture

William Massie, an architect and academic based in New York, is one such individual. His practice combines sophisticated CAM processes with off-the-shelf materials to produce complex geometries quickly and efficiently. He has also benefited from past experiences as a model maker – adopting digital 'working files' instead of construction drawings to make revisions faster and ensure a smooth transition between concept and execution. In recent years this workflow has given Massie the latitude to innovate with materials, appropriating some more common to modelmaking such as plastics and EPS foam, into designs for full scale buildings.

These novel approaches are most visible in the Big Belt House project (2000). The building's primary structure was built by CNC-milling sheets of expanded polystyrene foam to create formwork, which was then used to produce variegated, cast insitu concrete ribs. Once dry these ribs were raised into position, PVC piping was threaded through holes in them already created by the formwork, and finally insulating foam was sprayed over the exterior to create a sealed surface. This process was then repeated at an entirely different scale, with CNC-milling used to create everything from a mould for the sculptural kitchen sink, to the "transparent urethane gaskets into which the windows were set"[13]. Additionally, CAM was instrumental in the creation of steel jigs and templates to aid the laying out of the external walls, and the positioning of electrical and plumbing fittings in the concrete ground slab.

Massie also used the project to develop the 'puzzle piece' joint (interestingly compared by one writer with a traditional craftsman's dovetail joint) that affords several advantages: it permits rapid erection without fastening or adhering, reduces the need for

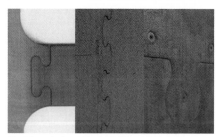

Massie's puzzle piece joint – applied in metal, wood and concrete.

SHoP's Porter House extension.

scaffolding, enables components to be assembled and checked in the workshop before being transported to site – and each one can be individualized to guarantee only one correct connection. Furthermore, like the routed moulds, the characteristics of CAM enabled the joint to easily cross divisions in material and scale – finding a use in "formwork, templating, sheathing, and connections of wood, steel and acrylic elements, whether for wall construction, window framing or furnishings"[14].

SHoP Architects

Another group exploring these issues are Sharples Holden Pasquarelli (SHoP) Architects – an American practice with a large portfolio of built work that investigates the emerging "common language between design and execution"[15]. Unlike Massie, however, SHoP rarely uses CAM to create intermediaries such as moulds or patterns, preferring instead to manufacture directly the structure, façade and interior elements they require, thus allowing them to consider vital material characteristics sometimes overlooked by others.

For example, the practice programmed the zinc panel system for their Porter House extension (2003) to incorporate standard material sizes and fabrication tolerances such as the bending radii of the metal, in an attempt to create an efficient structure that also avoids the monotony seen in repetitive panelled façades. This solution enabled them to reduce waste material to almost zero, as well as providing the group with fabrication procedures that they have adapted for latter work.

Elsewhere, the use of CAM in a lounge refurbishment (2004) at JFK airport gave SHoP tight control over the construction sequence, allowing them to simplify and accelerate fabrication. Nesting was used extensively to create "a 'just in time' approach that considered available lay-down space and ensured that all the parts needed to complete one group could be delivered, assembled and installed while the parts for the next group were being cut"[16]. In addition, by CNC-cutting the plastic parts that comprised the screens, SHoP could employ unskilled workers and avoid time-consuming tasks like sanding and finishing. The result is a design that creates considerable formal variation using only the most basic assembly and fixing systems.

Lounge refurbishment at JFK airport, by SHoP architects.

Rector Street bridge, by SHoP architects.

A similar approach was adopted for the Rector Street Bridge project (2002). Prompted by the events of September 11 2001, the bridge was needed immediately to reconnect areas around the World Trade Centre site that had become isolated from one another. As speed and order of construction were vital, SHoP opted for a prefabricated galvanized steel box-truss structure that could be erected at once, onto which they then fixed a series of perforated panels set at differing angles to offer or discourage views from the walkway. These panels were manufactured directly from digital files, thus enabling the architects to incorporate into their design sequencing, fixing and lay-down variables. The design, which was entirely finished within a few weeks, has proven extremely suitable for the location and just as significantly, can be disassembled with ease when the new World Trade Centre is finished.

The experiences of all these projects contributed to one of their most accomplished buildings to date – a camera obscura for Mitchell Park in New York (2005). Designed entirely within a digital environment, the building is "similar to an aircraft's fuselage...aluminium shelves [inside] serve as the formwork; guiding the shape and linking the structural integrity of the building with programmed display surfaces articulating the interior"[17]. The "logic of fabrication and erection processes" shown in the scheme was admirable – primary elements were laser cut and fabricated off site, before being transported to the park and slotted together to immediately form a datum onto which the rest of the structure could be attached[18]. Traditional plans and sections were rendered all but obsolete under this method, only produced to prove that the structure complied with zoning codes related to height and egress in fire. This has been a constant occupation of SHoP – a desire to use CAM techniques in order to eliminate the unnecessary "reductive analytic process of converting the three-dimensional concepts to two-dimensional representations which must then be reverse translated for construction"[19]. Doing so releases time that can then be reassigned elsewhere in other phases of design.

Frank Gehry

Obviously the changes occurring in modelling and manufacturing do not automatically guarantee us a stronger grasp of tectonics, or ensure more efficient construction methods. Even if it is diminishing rapidly, there is none the less still a certain amount of uncertainty separating what we wish to achieve and

Gehry's IAC building under construction.

what can be achieved with these technologies. This is aptly demonstrated in 3 different projects by Frank Gehry.

The first is a new science library (2005-) for Princeton University that presents itself as a series of interlocking steel elements, but which is in reality a traditional block and brick building clad in metal. This conflict between the undulating surfaces aspired to and the rectilinear solids their realization necessitated, has forced the contractors to adopt traditional time-consuming construction solutions in order to fix the different materials and geometries together.

Compare this to his design for the offices of the IAC company (2004-) in Lower Manhattan. Here Gehry has created an equally complex assemblage – this time of 5-storey volumes, each twisted 90 degrees horizontally, that together 'mimic the sails of boats in the harbour opposite'. Unlike the Princeton building, however, this one utilizes the advantages of CAM to create a clear correlation between the concept and its execution. Aware that the twisting would make standard glazing systems difficult to install, Gehry instead specified a series of concrete floor slabs supported on raked concrete columns, into

which unique mass-customized façade panels slot. This intelligent approach creates a building that encapsulates the sense of movement the architect desired without resorting to fussy construction solutions – on site each panel was locked into position smoothly and quickly by only 2 workers.

The final project by Gehry to consider is the DG Bank building's main conference centre (1995-2001). This 'Horse's Head', as it came to be known, was originally conceived for the Lewis residence, but following the project's cancellation was adopted as the centrepiece of this bank's atrium instead.

To aid its construction the architect built a 1:10 scale model, with which he could test materials and construction techniques for the real structure. It is thus a curious artefact – a mock-up that is at once both a crafted object, and template for the final high-tech structure. It is made up of a series of varying timber profiles arrayed along a linear path, through which secondary members are threaded to secure the structure (much like Massie's Big Belt House). Onto this are nailed hundreds of timber laths, then an outer skin of lead shingles. What is most interesting about this inhabitable maquette is the rough, uneven

Gehry's Horse's Head mock-up – there are noticeable irregularities in the outer lead cladding.

finish of its outer surface. For while it is unquestionably an impressive form from afar, up close the lapped lead panels noticeably distort from their intended shape and position.

Such issues reoccurred later on in the construction of the conference centre. Gehry experimented with different methods of fabrication, because the CNC-formed moulds needed to shape the stainless steel outer shell repeatedly shrank during their creation. Additionally these stainless steel panels proved difficult to machine-cut to the tolerance required. In the end each one had to be hand scribed and manually cut with a metal grinder – a method that resulted in "significant deviations in the final joints"[20]. As one project architect at Gehry's office notes, "a significant amount of on-site adjustment was required to get the desired appearance because the reality was different from the computer model"[21].

It is worth noting that the equally curvilinear interior of the conference centre suffered none of these problems. This wood cladding was instead completely hand-fabricated by a master carpenter who developed key construction details in situ with the architect, and perhaps more importantly was given "freedom to

modify these details during installation" based on his own experience[22].

Conclusions

These projects illustrate how the evolving technologies of Computer-Aided Manufacturing can facilitate a reengagement with material and tectonic concerns. The work of Massie, SHoP and Gehry all exhibit a strong understanding of the intricacies of construction – even though their designs reside in the immaterial, 'ephemeral' digital realm. William Massie's puzzle piece joint is one such example: a detail that changes its shape and dimensions in response to the different material characteristics of the wood, metal or plastic it is set within – yet at the same time the production of each connection is automated by the CAM routines he uses.

Furthermore, these projects suggest how we might achieve greater efficiency and reduce waste (SHoP), hasten construction time (Gehry) and transfer these technologies over to other fields of design (Massie). By utilizing all these advances in CAM together, architects can take greater control of the construction process – thereby reintegrating design and execution.

The advances in Computer-Aided Manufacturing discussed in the previous essay clearly have huge consequences for architecture. Of equal significance, however, are analogous developments occurring in digital modelling and analysis.

Over the last few decades basic CAD applications that were unable to represent much more than simplistic two dimensional relationships have been replaced by a series of progressively more sophisticated programs that can model and analyse complex three dimensional designs. Taking advantage of improvements in computing hardware, these programs now allow us to incorporate realworld attributes quickly and with a high level of precision into digital models. For example, diverse characteristics such as the physical (elasticity, rigidity), the visual (colour, reflectivity) and the environmental (wind flow, sound transmission, porosity) can now be simulated and analysed through them. In addition to aesthetic, structural and environmental concerns, these models can integrate many other factors. Cost can be estimated through the semi- or fully- automated production of bills of quantities, while programmatic analyses can be undertaken by calculating floor areas, circulation routes efficiencies, and so on. Even construction sequences or scaffolding

and formwork schedules can be produced through digital models. In short, the digital medium can facilitate the modelling and analysis of almost every aspect of architectural or structural design – and in many situations far more quickly and accurately than is possible manually.

These vast improvements in digital modelling, allied with the sophistication of current CAM technology, have a number of consequences beyond the 'narrow' issues of fabrication discussed in the previous essay.

This discussion will focus on how CAD and CAM are together changing the nature of collaboration, identity, workflow are many more topics in architecture today.

A Reshaping of Materiality

In the past the use of computers has been derided due to the perception that the work they produce is inherently immaterial in nature. We can now appreciate, however, that this disconnection was a result of the medium's immaturity at the time, rather than a fundamental property of it. Antoine Picon anticipated this development in a 2004 essay entitled "Architecture and the Virtual: Towards a New Materiality". In it

The extreme macro – planet earth revealed through geospatial software.

The extreme micro – glass under an electron microscope.

he dismisses the perceived gap between digital and analog design, arguing that the use of the computer does not "represent a substantial departure from the traditional features of architectural representation. Two-dimensional, hand-produced drawings are no more material than computer-based ones"[1].

Furthermore, because materiality is "to a large extent a cultural construction" and "we perceive the exterior world through the lenses provided...[by] technological culture", Picon feels the effect of the computer may "more accurately be described as a reshaping of, rather than an estrangement from, physical experience and materiality"[2].

The exact form this 'reshaping' of materiality takes is influenced by the twin forces of computation and globalization, that are together "destabiliz[ing] middle-range institutions and practices" by offering us perception at every scale – from the microscopic element up to the satellite view[3]. Picon believes this "short circuiting" of distance is shifting our expectations and making us at ease with a materiality that is

"increasingly defined at the intersection of two seemingly opposed categories. On the one hand is the totally abstract, based on signals and codes; on the other hand is the ultra concrete, involving an acute and almost pathological perception of material phenomena and properties such as light and texture as they are revealed by zoom-like practices" [4].

Certainly this changing definition of materiality, based as it is on "hybridization between the abstract and the ultra material", is borne out by the work of the different practicing architects discussed in the previous essay[5].

However, this explanation alone is not accepted by everyone. Others believe the defining factor in our changing perception of materiality is not this mediation offered by the computer during modelling, it is instead the introduction of CAM into the process. Picon himself has subtly acknowledged this, noting that "computer-aided material production seems to abolish the distance between representation and materiality"[6]. This idea is elaborated upon by a London firm called Sixteen*Makers, a group that focuses on designing through making, and particularly CAM's effects on this process. One of the group's members, Nicholas Callicott, argues that:

"When we use CAM software...

'Blusher' installation by Sixteen*Makers – fabricated using CAM technology.

The Lord's cricket ground Media Centre by Future Systems utilizes a semi-monocoque construction system.

we are in a sense neither making nor drawing, but are engaged only in an active reading of an authored function that differentiates surplus matter from our unique form. In contrast to existing definitions, making is no longer identified through that which is made alone, but becomes inseparable from the combined acts of its description and viewing...CAM has altered the process of describing architecture as much as the process by which it is made" [7].

Put simply, Callicott believes that the essentially sequential relationship established between representation, fabrication and the resulting form has given way to a more dialectical relationship in which the three inform and affect one another. As such our reading of materiality is now inextricably bound to the visual language used by computers to envisage it as well as the mechanical processes that instantiate it.

As these varying positions show, the exact form this 'reshaping' of our relationship with materiality takes is debatable. However there is no doubt that it is an important question for architecture, and one that will repeatedly arise - not least because of the periodic

introduction of new software and hardware systems that are the vectors for this change.

New Materials

This reshaping of materiality is only partially of a perceptive nature – there are also real changes occurring in the materials employed in architecture. Digital design has enabled us to envisage more complex geometries than previously thought possible, which has in turn initiated a search for new materials with which to build them. Branko Kolarevic notes that interest in "new geometric complexities...led to a renewed interest in surface or shell structures in which the skin absorbs all or most of the stresses. That in turn prompted a search for "new" materials, such as high-temperature foams, rubbers, plastics, and composites, which were until recently rarely used in the building industry" [8]. By appropriating from diverse fields like boat and aircraft construction architects have created a reciprocal relationship, in which "new geometries opened up a quest for new materials and visa-versa" [9].

Modelling and manufacturing techniques used in contemporary boatbuilding have transferred across to achitecture.

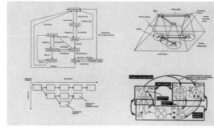

Relational models outside the profession of architecture – such as 'process management' and 'product management' used to evolve designs.

Identity, Authorship and Cross-Disciplinary Collaboration

The consequences of digital modelling and manufacturing techniques are not limited to the subjects of materiality and tectonics. Fundamental issues of identity and authorship are also now being re-examined in response to the computer's growing dominance. In the past design was reliant on time-consuming hand-drafted drawings, and was thus predisposed to a creative process that gradually and linearly consolidated a single concept. Digital design, however, allows for the simultaneous coexistence of multiple versions within one model, thus bringing into question the exact identity of the work produced. Ingeborg Rocker, Professor of Architecture at Harvard University, describes the problematic issue that arises from this:

"identity evolves and dissolves solely through the differential in-forming process, the repetition of difference throughout time. The object's formerly presumed unity dissolves as its versions, and the versions' relations, evolve. Subsequently, identity never becomes entirely comprehensible as it solely becomes a temporal, relational and hence incomplete remaining construct."[10]

Furthermore Rocker believes the "links and relationships" between these different variants now attain an almost equal status to them, as they provide the framework through which "predecessors and successors...[can] permutate – and hence constitute – the object differently each time"[11]. These complex interrelations can be kept track of through database-like information systems which provide a "revision history, an archive of past revisions that records the work's evolution over time"[12].

An excellent example of this is the BMW DynaForm pavilion (2001), a complex project that utilized two of these kinds of systems – software configuration management and engineering data management – to allow the project's "more than 75 architects, structural and mechanical engineers, communications experts, light designers and AV-media specialists to cooperate... simultaneously with one another"[13]. Using such systems ensured that the different design permutations were kept comprehensible yet could be incorporated into a single master design as required.

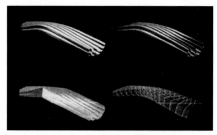
Iterative designs for Bernhard Franken's BMW pavilion.

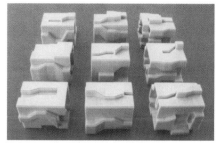
Variations quickly producing using rapid prototyping.

This project also shows the seemingly-inevitable next step once multiple identity design is introduced – the adoption of joint authorship, whereby different team members concurrently adapt and improve a single design, thereby taking fullest advantage of this technology. Multiple-authorship eschews the notion of a 'star architect', and instead encourages different individuals with different abilities to transfer in and out of projects as required.

The international collaborative SERVO, which has members in 3 different countries, bases its organizational structure on this premise: "collaboration means you must give up a certain amount of control. Rather than seeing this negatively, we embraced it and saw it as an opportunity"[14]. They argue this network organization model enables them to engage in projects that are unsuitable for "conventional or corporate models of architectural practice"[15].

Workflow

The conventional sequence of design has also been disrupted by digital modelling and manufacturing processes. Many stages of design (except for the initial sketch) can be completed faster by employing computers. For example, context models can be au-

tomatically constructed from topology and building datasets widely available on the internet. Similarly early schemes can be modelled and analysed quickly in a number of different ways, such as by producing singular components like doors and windows, and then duplicating them over a basic form. Lastly, rapid prototyping can be used to fabricate physical models of different designs quickly and with ease.

This combination of speed and minimum effort allows architects to explore design alternatives in a more 'risk free' manner – a possibility further supported by the ease with which digital models can be manipulated, saved in a certain state for return to later, and so on. Taken together these changes undermine the established order of design by permitting iterations and feedback loops that force practices to view design as "dynamical and nonlinear, and not as a process with a beginning, middle and end"[16].

The feedback that generates new designs does not necessarily have to be based on human intervention and interpretation. In a project for a redundant observatory sited within University College London, Sixteen*Makers produced an object that conflates architecture, sculpture and information systems, there-

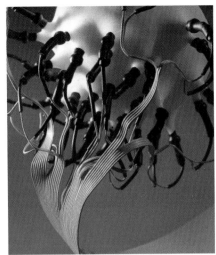

The installation in place within the observatory.

Sixteen*Makers installation at a disused observatory. The piece integrate electonics, product design and architecture.

by allowing them to semi-automatically evolve iterative designs for its form and function. Sited within a vacant telescope slot, this strange article is comprised of a hollow hemisphere (made through fused deposition modelling) inside of which are embedded an array of light-dependant sensors. Throughout the day prevailing winds turn an acrylic conduit atop this structure, intermittently activating different sensors and producing an "informal 'thumbprint' of the prevailing physical conditions" in the form of electronic data[17].

This 'thumbprint' is not simply illustrative, however. Sixteen*Makers wish it to be "generative... [they] seek to integrate the information with subsequent design proposals for the site"[18]. In this way the group can focus their attention "not simply on the object per se,

but on the processes that have gone into making that object and the reception of the object in situ"[19].

There is one final way in which the traditional sequence of design has been disrupted. When assessing the constructability of a complex form it is unwise to primarily rely on the "nearly instinctual visual evaluation process" that so often informs our decisions[20]. Instead we must withhold our judgement and utilize more accurate machine-based methods of assessment. As Andre Chaszar notes, "analyses of geometric properties such as curvature are of particular importance in assessing the constructability of complex shapes, for which the choice of material and fabrication process are more explicitly critical than for planar and orthogonal forms"[21]. As we produce increasingly complex forms in architecture, we will therefore find ourselves more often pushing designs beyond the con-

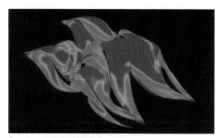

Curvature analysis of NOX's Son-O-House

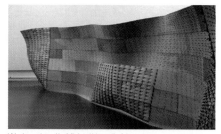

Work produced by Michael Hensel's AA students – showing how small scale rules (in this case the curvature of individual elements of wood) produce large scale effects.

ceptual stage, to the analytical stage in order to test its basic feasibility, and then back again in response to the results of this analysis.

Scales of Design

These technologies also afford us the ability to comfortably move both techniques and details between scales during design. Antoine Picon, we recall, anticipated this when he said we had greatly diminished the perceived distance between the macro and the micro.

We can clearly perceive this in William Massie's puzzle piece joint, a detail that easily migrates between scales – knitting together large structural elements, or individual floor planks, or even small items of furniture. Another example is the massive scale difference implicit in the work of Michael Hensel and the Emergence and Design Group at the Architectural Association. This group base their work on emergence theory, in which "agents residing on one scale start producing behaviour that lies one scale above them"[22]. Such movements from "low-level rules to higher-level sophistication" are present in every aspect of the world around us – dictating how "ants create colonies; urbanites create neighbourhoods... [and how] simple pattern-recognition software learns how to recommend new books"[23].

In Hensel's own work, for example, he has looked at how technologies like CAM and nano-fabrication could be used to create building elements with minute surface finishes similar to those seen on the underside of leaves. These panels would collectively have a similar environmental effect as the leaf – creating thousands of very small areas of pressure near them that together slow the air speed and therefore produces advantageous climatic conditions around a building.

New Tools

Of course many of these changes have been facilitated by our ability to create specific digital tools in the form of customized scripts and programs. Although there is simply not enough time here to discuss the full scope of this subject, there are a few basic points of interest worth considering.

Compared to manual drafting these tools offer us a far greater array of methods through which we can interact with the digital medium. However, with one or

One stage of Mark Burry's parametric model.

two noticeable exceptions, they also demand a higher level of involvement in order to make best use of them – "the range of choices and their effects far exceeds the consequences or the quandaries of earlier generations: pen or pencil...T-square or parallel rule?"[24]. Because of this the benefits of working digitally are not immediately apparent in the same way that they are in other media.

If we can overcome this initial uncertainty, however, these tools enable us to engage with projects that are unfeasible otherwise. This is illustrated by the parametric modelling work Mark Burry undertook on the rose window of Antoni Gaudi's Sagrada Familia (1882-). A traditional construction sequence (i.e. design then fabrication) could not be used as the project had a very tight timeframe, and more significantly the exact geometry of the two towers that frame the window was unknown. Instead Burry had to adopt a 'lean construction' approach, in which upper sections of the window were surveyed, designed and finalised at the same time as lower sections were installed in place and the scaffolding rose:

"While the lower quarter of

The completed Rose Window – note the uneven surfaces of the adjoining towers, which it had to smoothly and acurately meet.

the window was being constructed on site, the second quarter was still being cut in Galacia, the third quarter was made into templates in Australia to guide the stonemasons, and the design of the top quarter was being redefined in collaboration between the Sagrada Familia design office and the team in Australia[25].

This just-in-time form of architecture was made possible by the parametric software Burry employed, which allowed him to flexibly adjust his design in response to periodic new data from the survey – the associated geometries in the window simply realigned when any point or element moved. Clearly this level of expertise in software programming is beyond the ability of the majority of architects, however this example is still relevant to this discussion as it reveals the full potential of designing in the digital medium.

Conclusions

The conventional sequence of design is being replaced by a more adaptive process in which concepts are rapidly modelled, printed in 3D, physically altered, then re-imported, after which the cycle begins again. While it is clear that this sort of iterative method of work is not impossible using manual means, it is vastly less efficient without the involvement of the computer and CAM. Furthermore the design process can change from being a relatively private, individual affair to a truly collaborative one when such digital techniques are introduced. Models can be distributed over a network, allowing for many different people and many different disciplines to input into the process simultaneously. Governed properly, this could break down the divisions between architect, engineer, contractor and consultants – a change that can only improve the quality of the final buildings that result.

References

Redefining the Physical: The Architectural Implications of Computer-Aided Manufacture

01   Le Corbusier, (1923). *Vers Une Architecture*.
02   This table is an abbreviation of descriptions given on Page 120-122 - Kolarevic, B. (2005), *Designing and Manufacturing Architecture in the Digital Age*. [www.tkk.fi/events/ ecaade/ E2001presentations/ 05_03_kolarevic.pdf]
03   Page 279 – Kolarevic, B. (2001), *Manufacturing Digital Architectures*. [cumincades.scix.net/ data/ works/ att/ 483c.content.pdf]
04   Comment made during personal interview with Daniel Bosia on 22-09-06.
05   Page 122 – Kolarevic, B. (2005).
06   Page 71 – Gershenfield, N. (2005). FAB: *The Coming*

Revolution on your Desktop. Basic Books, New York. 0-465-02745-8.

07   See Sass, L. (2005), A Production System for Design and Construction with Digital Fabrication. [ddf.mit.edu/projects/ CABIN/ cabin_mit_2005.pdf]

08   Unused powder around the formed element also supports it – enabling overhangs and undercuts that might otherwise break.

09   Comment made during personal interview with Matthew Lewis on 29-09-06.

10   Page 32 – Slessor, C. (1997),'Atlantic star', Architectural Review, 102(12).

11   Page 9 – Gershenfield, N. (2005).

12   In 1951 the world's first commercial computer, Univac, came out – It weighed 8 tons.

13   Page 19 – Gilmartin, B. (2004), 'Merging design and making: Bill Massie', Praxis: New technologies: New Architectures, no. 6.

14   Page 205 – Chaszar, A. [ed](2006). Blurring the Lines: Computer-Aided Design and Manufacturing in Contemporary Architecture. Wiley Academy, Chichester. 0-470-86849-X.

15   Introduction on rear cover of Sharples, Holden, Pasquarelli / SHoP (2002), Architectural Design: Versioning: Evolutionary Techniques in Architecture, vol. 72, no. 5.

16   Page 32 – Sharples, (2006), 'Drawing in the digital age', Blurring The Lines.

17   Page 34 – Sharples, (2006).

18   Page 29 – Sharples, (2006).

19   Page 31 – Sharples, (2006).

20   Page 66 – Takemori, T. (2006), 'Conference Hall, DZ Bank, Berlin', Blurring The Lines.

21   Page 67 – Takemori, (2006).

22   Page 64 – Takemori, (2006).

Further Implications of CAM and CAD in Contemporary Architecture

01   Page 115 – Picon, A. (2004), 'Architecture and the virtual', Praxis: New technologies: New Architectures, no. 6.

02   Page 115 – Picon, A. (2004).

03   Page 119 – Picon, A. (2004).

04   ibid.

05   ibid.

06   Page 120 – Picon, A. (2004).

07   Page 68 – Callicott, N. (2005), 'Adaptive architectural design', Architectural Design: Design through Making, jun.

08   Page 279-280 – Kolarevic (2001).

09   Page 280 – Kolarevic (2001).

10   Page 12 – Rocker, I (2002), 'Evolving architectures - dissolving identities', Architectural Design: Versioning: Evolutionary Techniques in Architecture, vol. 72, no. 5.

11   Page 13 – Rocker, I (2002).

12   ibid.

13   Page 12 – Rocker, I (2002).

14   Page 140 – SERVO (2003), 'Design Intelligence', A+U, may-aug.

15   ibid.

16   Page 6 – Speaks, M. (2002), 'Preface', Architectural Design: Versioning: Evolutionary Techniques in Architecture, vol. 72, no. 5.

17   Page 80 – Callicott, N. (2005).

18   ibid.

19   Page 25 – Till, J. (2001), 'Sixteen*Makers', Architectural Design: Young Blood, April.

20   Page 12 – Chaszar, A. [ed](2006).

21   ibid.

22   Page 15 – Johnson, S. (2001). Emergence: The Connected Lives of Ants, Brains, Cities and Software. Penguin books, London. 0-713-99400-2.

23   ibid.

24   Page 13 – Chaszar, A. [ed](2006). The intuitive software referred to here is SketchUp.

25   Page 11 – Stacey, M. (2005), Digital Fabricators. [www.fabrication.ald.utoronto.ca/ exhibitions/ digital_fabricators/ digital_fabricators_catalogue.pdf]

This essay provides a brief introduction to parametric design.
A brief historical outline demonstrates that this approach is
not new, but is rather allowing design ideas which have been
pursued for centuries to be undertaken to a far greater level of
ambition and speed. An example of a recent project undertaken
by the author gives an hands-on explanation of its application.

Translating Design Intent

In 1997 in *Translations from Drawing to Building* Robin Evans wrote of the ambiguous nature of the separation of the built work of architecture and its conception. This article briefly explores how the separation proposed by Evans is currently being reduced through the introduction of new technology to the field of architectural design. In this context, *translating* is the process of converting architectural design ideas into expressions that define relationships and dependencies in digital architectural geometry. These methods are known as 'parametric design'. One of the results of this field is the production of digital data that allows direct fabrication of building components and therefore reducing the separation of the design process and the production of built form. This process is illustrated with a case study where the author has acted as parametric consultant on The New Irish Stadium on Lansdowne Road in Dublin.

Parametric Tools

Parametric and associative tools enable mathematical definitions of two and three dimensional architectural models. A parametric model can be defined as a set of rules configured by a series of parameters or variables; this is in opposition to previous modes where discrete numerical values define the model. The associative nature of parametric systems enables the construction of geometric relationships between objects. These relationships allow for design development or mathematical modelling of both abstract conceptual notions and material construction constraints.

A parametric model can be regarded as a dynamic decision making or problem solving device, as the model provides a mechanism for exploring design ideas. The geometric and numeric data embedded in the model can be extracted and used to inform the design decisions, making the model a storage vessel for information. The parametric model can also act as a generative tool where the configuration of a model may be unanticipated when a series of rule sets are combined.

A brief history of rule based design in architecture

At the core of working using a parametric method is the use of rules. The earliest use of rule based techniques is evident in stereotomy, the process of cutting solids such as stone. The first built examples are in the masonry structures of arches, sloping barrel vaults and groin vaults of ancient civilisations in Egypt, Greece and Rome. It was not until 1486-1490 when Mathes Roriczer (a master mason) and Hanns Schmuttermayer (a goldsmith), published booklets

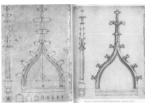
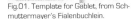

Fig.01. Template for Gablet, from Sch-muttermayer's Fialenbuchlein.

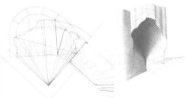

Fig 02 The trait for the trompe at Anet and perspective projection. From Robin Evans. Translations from Drawing to Building

Fig 03 Section of Sagrada Familia and inverted image of hanging chain model.

that were non-philosophical texts describing procedural techniques for the production of particular artefacts[Fig.01]. The methods described were extrapolation devices or templates for deriving elevation from plan.

In the sixteenth century the process of stereotomy became more exact. The rule based process of gothic stereotomy was extended through an understanding of Euclidean geometric methods and projective drawing techniques. The work of the French Renaissance Architect Philibert de L'Orme provides illustration of this. In de L'Orme's book *Premier Tome de L'Architecture* he provides descriptions of projective drawing methods procedures that result in a set of drawings that describe the length and angles for the templates for stones. De L'Orme refers to these as *traits* [Fig. 02]. The trait is essentially a rule based drawing procedure, adjustment to the inputs, the plan and section, working through the successive prescribed orthogonal projections would result in a different set of cutting patterns and therefore ultimately a different physical product. So far examples of rule based design thinking use only geometric rules developed through in-situ constructive methods or drawn projective procedures. More recently, Gaudi's design methods for the Sagrada Famila in Barcelona included more complex

geometric methods than those previously described. Much of the masonry is a result of the application of methods for creating ruled surface geometry to create hyperbolic paraboloid, helicoid and hyperboloid surfaces. The form of the columns and vaulting at the Sagrada Familia and the vaulting of Colonia Guell Crypt can also be regarded as the product of rule based methods. In these cases the geometric rules involved are driven by physical rules rather than rules applied by the designer. These structural forms are the result of the construction of physical models known as hanging chain or catenary systems [Fig 03].The work of Frei Otto in the later part of the 20th century can be seen to extend the idea of physical computation as illustrated in the projects by Gaudi above. In addition to hanging chain or net models [Fig 04] Otto also worked with tent structures (stretch fabric and net models), soap films (minimal surfaces), pneumatic devices, spoil cones or sand piles and thread models (minimal path). Each of these physical modelling processes can be thought of as taking a set of physical rules forces and applying them to a particular material to generate a specific geometry. Detailed measurements of these models would then be taken in order to construct the structure as illustrated in Fig 04, the String hanging chain model.

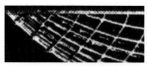

Fig 04 String hanging chain model.

Fig 05. Aerial view of proposed design for Lansdowne Road Stadium, Dublin. Credit HOK Sport

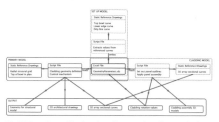

Fig 06. Lansdowne Road project diagram of problem and sub-problems.

Fig 07. Radial array of planar curves

Fig 08. Geometry of planar sectional curve

Subdivision of Labour

A history of rule based methods in architectural design serves a dual purpose; the first to demonstrate how fundamental they are in architectural design; and the second to illustrate the gradual subdivision of labour in the construction industry. At the origin of this second thread the builder both designs and builds with little premeditation but following known methods. The first split occurs between the designer and the builder. The designer draws what he what he sees as the means to communicate his ideas to the builder and the separation between architect and built work begins. This first divide in construction roles necessitate a formularisation of the process of orthographic drawing methods. The next split occurs with the establishment of methods relating to structural design, and the role of the engineer emerges.

Further subdivision of roles in the process of construction can be observed as the rules relating to other specialised tasks become formulated. Until we arrive at the contemporary design team. The benefits to the multifaceted modern team are clear, however at each split the architect's role becomes more of managing the process, the built form being shifted further from his hands. Underlying each specialised role in the construction industry is the geometry of the building. The parametric tool offers a means to controlling this core shared information and therefore directly reconnecting the designer with the production of the built object or artefact. In order to truly capitalise on this new technology the architect must have some control of the control of the parametric model and therefore an understanding of the principles of parametric design – rule based thinking, problem solving and computer programming.

Parametric Modelling of Lansdowne Road National Stadium

The brief was to produce a parametric model to define the geometry of a wrapped cladding skin for a stadium which functions as both roof to the seating bowl and façade as well as for accommodation beneath the bowl. A detailed proposal for both roof and façade cladding strategy was also required.

The geometry defined an interface between the remit of architectural work (cladding the form) and the design of the roof structure. The skin geometry was defined through close collaboration with Buro Happold, the engineers responsible for design of the roof structure. The parametric definition of the skin used by HOK was extended by Buro Happold to include a parametric definition of the structure. In this way geometric changes could be immediately incorporated into the process of structural design.

Planning permission for the stadium had been granted based on a design submission using mainly traditional architectural drawing and modelling methods. The proposed design is for a new 50,000 seat facility on the existing ground. The final design is informed by a highly constrained site; planning restrictions relating to rights to light issues of surrounding residential buildings, a maximum building height and a railway station on the edge of the site. The three-dimensional geometry of the drip line (the inner edge of the roof) had been defined through a series of daylight studies that ensured the growth of natural grass on the pitch. A further factor that had influenced the form of the skin was a three-dimensional curve from the back of the seating bowl this had been defined using a software that formed a part of the *Microstation* package.

Sectional Definition

The proposed method of geometric definition took its lead from the structural design. This consisted of an array of radial vertical planes each containing a curve which defined the tertiary members of the roof structure [Fig 07]. It was decided these sectional curves should be used to define the surface geometry. This process would also produce offset two-dimensional data for the tertiary structural sections.

Each of these sections would consist of three basic geometric objects 2 arcs and a straight line all in the same plane and each meeting the next tangentially. The elements were named SideArc, FilletArc and RoofLine [Fig 08]. The configuration of each sectional element would be defined by point data, corresponding with the position of tertiary planes, extracted from the original stadium model. The sectional curves are planar therefore can be defined by horizontal and vertical components. A series of basic geometric rules were established in order to define sectional curves.

Sectional Rules

1. The centre point of the SideArc would be at a constant level (level 6). The extent of the building in plan would therefore not exceed the plan at level 6.

2. The SideArc radius would be a constant.

3. The SideArc would pass through the plan curve of level 1.

4. The SideArc would end at a level that corresponded with the back of bowl curve.

5. The FilletArc would pass through a point a constant dimension above the back of bowl curve. This allowed the head height of the last row of seating and structural depth.

6. The origin for each tertiary plane would be located where the plane intersected the level 1 boundary curve.

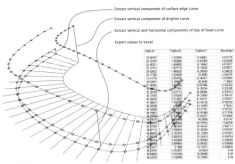

Extract vertical component of surface edge curve

Extract vertical component of dripline curve

Extract vertical and horizontal components of top of bowl curve

Export values to excel

Fig 09. Numeric extraction.

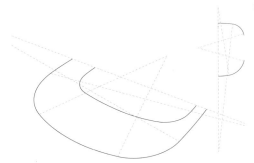

Fig 10. Drip line and first floor extent curves in plan.

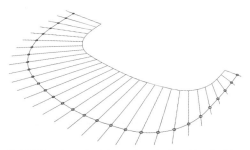

Fig 11. Referencing sectional planes and constructing origins of radial sections

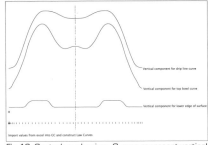

Fig 12. Control mechanism. Curves represent vertical
-behaviour of driver curves.

Control Curves (Law Curves)

Given the rules above, three points are required to configure each curve; a point at the lower outer edge of the surface, a point from the back of bowl curve, and a point at the drip line. Other than the lower surface edge these parts of the model had been previously defined by extensive studies relating to seating capacity and natural light levels on the pitch, these are referred to as driver curves.

Three-dimensional curves corresponding to these parts of the original model were extracted from HOK's original model and referenced into the parametric modelling application *Generative Components* [Fig 09]. Planes corresponding to the tertiary structural planes were constructed and intersected with the driver curves to create an array of points. The Z values (or vertical component) of these points were written as a spreadsheet. In the model overview this process is referred to as the set up model.

Horizontal variation of these three-dimensional curves was input to the model as three curves in plan. The extents of the first floor and drip line were constructed by creating a user defined feature, consisting of eight tangential arcs [Fig 10]. The first floor and drip

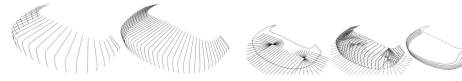

Fig 13. Increaseing the number of radial sections for definition of cladding sub frame.

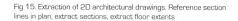

Fig 15. Extraction of 2D architectural drawings. Reference section lines in plan, extract sections, extract floor extents

Fig 14. Control of fillet radius.

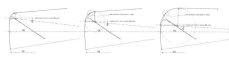

line curves are created as instances of this feature. The feature takes nine variables as inputs to define the radii of the arcs and their position relative to the model origin. These parameters are stored and read from the spreadsheet. The back of bowl curve was referenced in as a static drawing [little variation was anticipated with this element]. Finally a structural grid drawing is referenced into the model [Fig 11].

By intersecting this grid with the extents of the first floor level in plan the origin planes for the sections are defined. In order to construct the geometry for the proposed structural system for the cladding, the array of tertiary curves needed to be subdivided to provide intermediate support for panels. Essentially this means creating a higher resolution array of curves. The values extracted from HOK's model correspond with tertiary structural planes. Therefore a method was needed that would allow interpolation of these values so intermediate curves for the cladding substructure could be constructed [Fig 13].

The values extracted from HOK's model are used to construct a two-dimensional control curve that describes the vertical behaviour of each driver curve as

we move from North to South around the stadium [Fig 12]. Two additional law curves were constructed; one for determining the horizontal component of the back of bowl curve and a second that allows the level of the back of bowl to be dropped. The horizontal component of the back of bowl is determined by measuring a distance between points where the structural grid intersects the and first floor curve and the back of bowl curve. The latter control curve takes advantage of what is essentially an arbitrary rule; the correspondence of the end of the SideArc with the level of the back of bowl. By allowing adjustment here the user gains additional control of the radius of the FilletArc and we have an aesthetic control mechanism [Fig 14].

Two-Dimensional Output

Built into the model are two mechanisms for extracting two dimensional drawing data. These enable sections corresponding to a grid related to the seating bowl structure and the extents of floor plates to be extracted. In order to extract these, the composite curve array is lofted to create a bspline surface. A series of vertical planes are defined using the seating bowl grid and horizontal planes at each floor level.

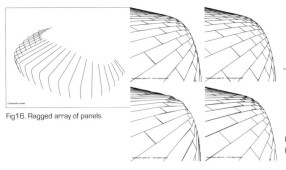

Fig16. Ragged array of panels

Fig 18. User defined features for showing water run off from panels and panels exceeding a specified out of plane dimension.

Fig 17. Visual comparison of torqued and planar panel systems

Using the drawing extraction feature in Generative Components curves at the intersection of the surface and planes can be extracted as two dimensional drawings and saved into a set of individual drawing files, which were then referenced into the two dimensional architectural drawings [Fig 15].

Panelling ProcessThree-Dimensional Output

One of the key aspects to the design of the parametric model was the subdivision of the tertiary structural planes. This is three-dimensional output that provides the definition of sub-framing for the panelling system. A list of values in the parameter spreadsheet defines the number of subdivisions for each tertiary bay. In the initial panelling studies a one dimensional list of points was equally spaced along each of the resulting radial curves from the subdivision. Each radial curve is of different length, therefore the result is a ragged two dimensional point grid this is then used to define individual panels [Fig 16].

Using this method for creating a point grid early studies explored various options for panel setting out, these included comparison between the use of pla-

nar and torque panels [Fig 17]. Devices (user defined features) were constructed and tested that graphically illustrated drainage directions across panels and flagged panels that exceeded a maximum out of plane dimension (hypothetically defined by manufacturer's specification for the chosen material) [Fig 18].

The project cladding team used these studies in meetings with a shortlist of cladding contractors drawn up to tender for the cladding package. These meetings eventually converged on a strategy which defined general rules for setting out and type of material for the cladding. The skin was divided into two distinct zones a façade area which would be a rainscreen system and the roof area which would have a sealed system. The division between these two zones corresponded with the top of the edge truss of the roof structure this also corresponded with the start of the filleting arc of the surface curves.

All cladding contractors favoured a planar system. The profile of the panels was detailed to tolerate the appearance of gaps between adjacent panels due to the forced planarity. To achieve this each panel was

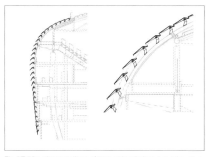

Fig 17. Visual comparison of torqued and planar panel systems

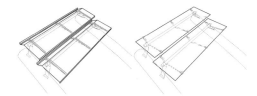

Fig 17. Visual comparison of torqued and planar panel systems

formed from a folded polycarbonate profile, and would be supported in a standardised bracket [Fig 20]. Using the surface curves to define the cladding panels would be of standard width but varied length a typical panel would be 1.2m x 3.75m. Similar details were used for both the roof and façade systems.

An additional factor for the façade area was that some panels would have a fixed position which would vary between fully open and closed. This would satisfy a certain ventilation area requirement for large air handling units. The design team had proposed that these open areas should be blended into the façade so that panels adjacent to the open area would be slightly open. An experimental version of this potential was demonstrated prior to the final panel setting out.

Once these more specific requirements were known the parametric panelling strategy was revisited. In developing a fully resolved cladding solution the architects were able to show a detailed design intent which demonstrates the principle to cladding contractors. This helped reduce the tendered cost of the package and allow the architectural design team to

retain aesthetic control. The parametric model also provides precise three dimensional models that are used to produce accurate visualisation material which is of great importance in describing the design to all involved [Fig 24].

Following a series of test studies on the technique for accurately setting out the panels, a method for defining equal widths was discovered [Fig 22]. Techniques for controlling the rotation were tested the most successful was to create a spreadsheet each cell represented one panel and contained a value that defined the angle of rotation [Fig 21].

During these test studies it was decided that the output of the panelling function should be a grid of *Microstation* shape features. These would act as a place holder device that could be later used to apply a detailed component from the actual panel assembly. The final output could then be used for checking the system worked in terms of the proposed detailing system and for the visualisation of the system.

Bays	81	82	83	84	85	86	87	88	89	90	91	92	93	94	95	96	97
ID Tag	0	1	2	3	4	5	6	7	8	9	0	1	2	3	4	5	6
0	13.0913	13.5427	13.5427	13.2719	13.0084	12.7463	12.4914	12.2416	11.9967	11.7568	11.5217	11.2912	11.0654	10.8441	10.6272	10.3616	10.1025
1	15.7096	16.2513	16.2513	15.9262	15.6077	15.2955	14.9897	14.6899	14.3961	14.1081	13.8260	13.5495	13.2765	13.0129	12.7526	12.4338	12.1230
2	18.8515	19.5015	19.5015	19.1115	18.7293	18.3547	17.9876	17.6278	17.2753	16.9298	16.5912	16.2594	15.9342	15.6155	15.3032	14.9206	14.5475
3	22.6216	23.4016	23.4018	22.9338	22.4751	22.0256	21.5851	21.1534	20.7303	20.3157	19.9094	19.5112	19.1210	18.7386	18.3638	17.9047	17.4571
4	27.1481	28.0822	28.0822	27.5206	26.9701	26.4307	25.9021	25.3841	24.8764	24.3789	23.8913	23.4135	22.9452	22.4863	22.0366	21.4957	20.9466
5	32.5754	33.6995	33.0047	32.3642	31.7189	31.0828	30.4609	29.8517	29.2546	28.6696	28.0982	27.5343	26.9836	26.4439	25.7839	25.1382	
6	39.0904	40.4384	49.4384	39.6296	38.8370	38.0803	37.2991	36.5531	35.8222	35.1096	34.4039	33.7154	33.0411	32.3903	31.7327	30.9763	30.1659
7	46.9065	48.5260	48.5260	47.5555	46.6046	45.6723	44.7589	43.8637	42.9864	42.1267	41.2842	40.4585	39.6493	38.9563	38.0782	37.1272	36.1990
8	53.0597	55.4593	55.4593	54.3402	53.2522	52.1869	51.1530	50.1296	49.1273	48.1446	47.1819	46.2383	45.3135	44.4072	43.5191	42.4311	41.3703
9	59.5604	61.8204	61.8204	60.3880	59.1932	57.9956	56.8397	55.6999	54.5855	53.4942	52.4243	51.3758	60.3453	49.3414	48.3645	47.1487	45.9570
10	64.5815	67.2222	66.8772	64.6920	63.2690	62.0036	60.7636	59.5483	58.3573	57.1902	56.0464	54.8254	53.8266	52.7604	51.4316	50.1459	
11	70.5899	73.3333	73.3333	71.6667	70.4280	69.0207	67.6403	66.2675	64.9816	63.6625	62.3893	61.3415	59.9187	58.7203	57.5459	56.1072	54.7048
12	77.3333	80.0000	80.0000	78.4000	76.6320	78.2954	73.7586	72.3137	70.8874	69.4900	68.0610	66.6688	65.3658	64.0588	62.7773	61.2079	59.8777
13	70.8889	73.3333	73.3333	71.6667	70.4290	69.0207	67.6403	66.2675	64.9816	63.6525	62.3893	61.1415	59.9187	58.7203	57.6317	56.2118	54.8414
14	64.9815	67.2222	66.8778	64.9832	63.2690	62.0036	60.7636	59.5483	58.3573	57.1902	56.0464	54.9254	53.8269	52.9077	51.7357	50.5818	
15	59.5604	61.8204	61.8204	60.3880	59.1932	57.9956	56.8397	55.6999	54.5855	53.4942	52.4243	51.3758	60.3453	49.3414	48.3645	47.0777	45.9655
16	54.6025	56.4853	56.4853	55.3556	54.2485	53.1635	52.1003	51.0583	50.0371	49.0364	48.0556	47.0945	46.1526	45.2298	44.1836	43.1262	42.8708
17	50.0523	51.7763	51.7762	50.7427	49.7239	46.7353	47.7586	46.8034	45.8973	44.9500	44.0610	43.1700	42.3066	41.4605	40.5349	40.1067	39.4684
18	46.8813	47.4634	47.4634	46.5141	45.5838	44.6721	43.7787	42.9031	42.0451	41.2042	40.3801	39.5728	36.7810	36.0054	37.8796	36.9576	36.3365
19	42.0676	43.5081	42.6378	41.7862	40.9495	40.1306	39.3279	38.5413	37.7705	37.0161	36.2748	36.5469	34.8363	34.4993	33.9774	33.4502	
20	38.5530	39.8824	39.0846	38.3031	37.5370	36.7863	36.0505	35.3290	34.6229	33.9305	33.2519	32.5868	31.9351	31.6715	31.2373	30.7973	
21	35.3403	36.5590	35.6599	36.8277	35.1112	34.4069	33.7206	33.0493	32.3854	31.7377	31.1029	30.4809	29.8713	29.2736	29.0755	28.7181	28.3530
22	32.3952	33.5123	33.5123	32.8421	32.1652	31.5415	30.9107	30.2925	29.6866	29.0923	28.5110	27.9406	27.3820	26.8349	26.5043	26.0322	28.1028
23	29.6598	30.7196	30.7196	30.1052	29.5031	28.9131	28.2348	27.7681	27.2127	26.6685	26.1351	25.6124	25.1003	24.5960	24.5043	24.2739	24.0311
24	27.2210	28.1597	27.5965	27.0445	26.5036	25.9736	25.4541	24.9450	24.4461	23.9572	23.4780	23.0085	22.5483	22.4958	22.3154	22.1239	
25	24.9526	25.8130	25.8130	25.2986	24.7960	24.2960	23.5060	23.3329	22.9083	22.4089	21.9908	21.5215	21.0915	20.6659	20.6159	20.5156	20.3680
26	22.8732	23.6815	23.6819	23.1887	22.7246	22.2794	21.6250	21.3359	20.9607	20.5416	20.1397	19.7281	19.3335	18.9466	18.9591	18.9513	18.7515
27	20.9671	21.5901	21.8901	21.3563	20.9312	20.4145	20.0063	19.5061	19.2140	18.8297	18.4531	18.0841	17.7224	17.3679	17.4051	17.3452	17.2633
28	19.2198	19.8826	19.6826	19.4649	19.0952	18.7913	18.3391	17.9723	17.6120	17.2606	16.9154	16.5771	16.2455	15.9206	15.9784	15.9416	15.8932
29	17.6182	18.2257	18.2257	17.8512	17.5040	17.1529	16.8108	16.4746	16.1451	15.0222	15.5068	15.1909	14.8917	14.5939	14.6987	14.6562	14.6516
30	16.1530	16.7069	16.7069	16.3728	16.0453	15.7244	15.4099	15.1017	14.7997	14.5037	14.2136	13.9293	13.6508	13.3777	13.4664	13.4742	13.4706
31	14.8042	15.3147	15.3147	15.0084	14.7082	14.4140	14.1258	13.8432	13.5664	13.2950	13.0291	12.7596	12.5132	12.2629	12.3638	12.3876	12.4015

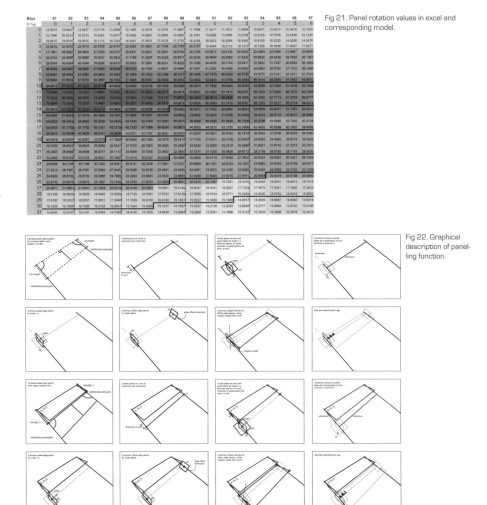

Fig 21. Panel rotation values in excel and corresponding model.

Fig 22. Graphical description of panel-ling function.

Fig 23. Five cladding bays with panel assembly components.

Fig 24. Detail of rendered image created using parametric cladding output. Credit HOK Sport.

The geometry produced, as Microstation shapes, by the panelling function is saved as a static drawing and then referenced into another Generative Components script file where panel components can be applied. Due to the processing intensity this was carried out in small steps. A series of user defined features were created for each of the elements of the panel assembly plus some alternative designs were developed. The assembly of the panel was broken into the following parts each with further variables for their definition:

Fig 25. Visualisation of stadium elevation.

• Polycarbonate profiled panel
• Planar glass panel
• Clamps to attached glass panel to brackets
• Fixing or rotation axis
• Brackets to fix axis to mullions
• Brackets to fix glass panel to axis
• Strap fixed brackets to attach panel to axis
• Point fixed brackets to attach panel to axis

A full scale mock up of the cladding system which was approved by the client, was built on the site in Dublin in November 2006 [Fig 26]. Demolition is due to begin during 2007 and construction later in the year.

Fig 26. Cladding mock up rig and detail.

3_ interviews

Facades of Recent Projects.
An interview with Alison Brooks
of Alison Brooks Architects.

AB -   Alison Brooks
JD -   Jeg Dudley

JD

How did the facades evolve for your recent project in Wandsworth?

AB

The Herringbone houses timber façades came about primarily due to the site context – it is a backland site that was densely populated with trees and formed a backdrop to the South London Bowls Club. Our approach was to integrate the buildings into this context through the use of timber cladding. To expand on the language and detailing of timber that we had used in earlier projects we came up with the idea of taking a herringbone pattern of flooring and extending it through to the exterior of the house - wrapping it in a pattern that you would normally find on floors. It's slightly tongue in cheek, but it also has references to the use of brick in Tudor construction, which use post and beam construction with a herringbone brick infill. That wasn't the immediate frame of reference, but once you do something experimental that is playful and pushes the boundary in one sense, it suddenly leads you to make connections with things that you wouldn't normally associate with what you are doing - it's a kind of serendipity.

JD

Although each house has a clearly defined volume, the manner in which these surfaces wrap to become at once both horizontal and vertical, internal and external, means that you perceive it more as a house made of surfaces. You've talked in the past about these buildings being "conceived as an assembly of planar elements as opposed to 'punched' masonry".

AB

Planes rather than rooms or volumes, yes. The advantage of using herringbone was that it also creates the optical illusion of a more three dimensional or faceted form than what is actually there.

We were really limited in terms of what we could do with the building forms - mainly by the Planning Department and the demands of neighbours on adjacent properties - who wanted to preserve views through the canopy of trees and keep the impression of pavilions in a woodland. Although most of the woodland has disappeared now because it the trees were quite unhealthy, we liked the idea of creating buildings that could be camouflaged among the trunks and branches of trees, that would have this more faceted and three dimensional appearance even though they are

 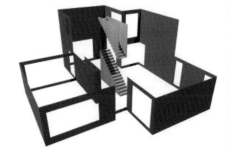

Volumetric views of houses

quite strong rectilinear forms.

The scheme also pushes craftsmanship a little bit - the reason that boarding is usually horizontal or vertical is that it's quick and easy to put up, although it still requires a fair degree of control. Whereas the herringbone required quite a bit more effort.

JD

On the junctions like edges and corners?

AB

Certainly on edges and corners, but also setting out all the basic lines and cutting the timber - but because we were working with such simple forms, the client was willing to go the extra mile and do something unusual with the cladding.

JD

Were the parts manually cut out and dependent on drawings, or were the pieces made with computer-controlled machinery?

AB

Well, we had to set everything out really carefully, but the contractor had all the lengths pre-cut. There are left-handed and right handed versions, but all the strips of timber were 650mm long and cut at 23 degrees. A fair amount of cutting was done in the factory and then boards were brought to the site ready to be fixed in place. Each board had to be plugged - the screws are counter-sunk - and the counter-sunk holes were prefabricated too. What we find is that contractors tend to really like the projects we are doing because they are challenged and it does become a kind of showcase for their skill - especially the carpenters.

The contractor for Wrap House used to be a boat builder, and he just couldn't wait to get his hands on it, because it was an opportunity for him to show his stuff.

JD

Is there quite a lot of dialogue between yourselves and individuals like that? Do you encourage them to get involved and talk to you about how might be the best way to achieve projects?

AB

Obviously on small projects you do have a more direct relationship with the contractor and other people who are doing things. For example, on Fold House and Wrap House and other extensions, you have one-on-one conversations with the builder, whereas with the Herringbone Houses we didn't really know who the carpenters were, just because there were so many of them on site. But we tend to draw everything to death, so they have to produce it the way we draw it - I suppose there isn't that much discussion! I mean, there is a certain amount, but everything's clearly drawn because we also want to make it easy for them - we know we are kind of pushing it, so we had better make it as easy as possible, otherwise it's going to get sliced out of the project or compromised somehow. It is a tricky thing to achieve this balance between experimentation, compromise and craftsmanship.

JD

And inevitably there is also an artist's sensibility informing you work, because of your background working with Ron Arad.

AB

Well I ran the architectural arm of Ron Arad Associ-

Front view of houses

3D view of cladding

ates - so I did have the advantage of having an artist's viewpoint influencing me. From the minute I started working with Ron he was very unconventional in his approach to anything architectural - he was free of all the standards and norms and conventions that architects are usually burdened with - or at least were fifteen years ago.

I became intimately familiar with materials, with steel fabrication, and so on. Basically the idea that you can make anything - everything doesn't have to come from a catalogue or off the shelf. Actually, most of what we see in the built environment is hand made, we sort of get this idea that it's machine made but actually there's still craft everywhere. Even the panels that form the sides of the tube trains on the London Underground are partially hand beaten and hand welded, and then the welds are ground off. But you look at them and think, 'these are machine made'.

JD

The Herringbone Houses seem to be the latest stage in a series of projects - after Wrap House, Slope House and Fold House that explores the idea of flowing surfaces. In the past you've described the Fold House as a surface which is "extremely two dimensional, even

when it's three dimensional it's like working with origami, it's about expressing weightlessness". In contrast the Slope House is a surface too, but it's very clearly expressed as a "vertical extrusion of the landscape" - one has a definite thickness and weight.

AB

In a way that's true - I think they are all evolutions or variations on this idea of wrapping space, rather than carving space out of a volume and making rooms. It may have started with the Miesian or Breuer-esque approach where walls are always freestanding planes that shoot from the inside to the outside, and are somewhere between landscape and architecture. I've always been interested in the idea of continuity - how the wrapping of a building doesn't need to be restricted to the exterior, you can manipulate that surface and bring it inside the house and just develop rules for how you use or alter that plane. For example, with the Fold House we literally started with a flat sheet of paper, then cut it and folded it so that we created columns and chairs, and so on - all out of a single sheet. So you establish these rules - they're kind of like games - which are quite easy to apply at the scale of a pavilion, or a single storey extension, but get much harder when you get into multi-storey projects or something

3D view of cladding

with a more complex brief. It becomes more difficult to maintain the purity of that concept, and sometimes you just have to give up! You are sort of defeated by these restrictions you've created, and you tell yourself 'at this point it's okay if I break them'.

But in projects like the Hide House the surface is more about creating frames - each façade of the house, including the roof, is a trapezoidal or five-sided opening that frames a view of the landscape. So there was a different rule we set out for that project: that every façade was a kind of frame - it still isn't carving a solid, but it's not necessarily wrapping either.

JD

The form of that building suggests that it could be made from a single homogenous material like concrete, rather than an assembled skin, which would also help you when creating the flowing double and triple height spaces that occur in many of your designs.

AB

To be honest I'm not that interested in making a building out of a single material - as Le Corbusier did with the Chapel at Ronchamp, using concrete on the inside and the outside. In a way I think that's an old school Modernist ideal. It's so limiting as it's really hard to build - especially in concrete - and have a fair-faced finish on the inside and outside, with insulation inside. It's also really expensive, impossibly expensive.

I think it's more interesting to think of a surface as a skin that is free to be structural or non-structural, depending on what you want it to do, and have that ability to peel it away from an inner core material, or to wrap around another surface. In a project for a house that we are doing in Tunbridge Wells it's mainly zinc cladding, but with certain walls and the fireplace and other pieces in stone. Basically the zinc cladding wrapped around the outside of the house and came in, sometimes just forming an edge or lining to a massive material like stone or concrete. I think that contrast between the skin and the other materials of the house is potentially as interesting, or more interesting, than trying to get that purity where the whole form or entire planar surface is just one material. It inevitably becomes too thick, you can't help it.

However we have done a few projects recently that deliberately express that thickness. Our competition entry for Corpus Christi College, Oxford, was clad in stone, and the concept was that it emerges from the gardens of the college like any other stone building that has mass and presence, but it is carved in a way that makes it more weightless and lighter. The main body of the building is inside this element which was the garden wall, and our concept was to take that wall and stretch it and fill the space in between with program so that it basically looks the same as what was there before, but it has become inhabited. Unfortunately we didn't win that, but it carried on some of the themes that we are still pursuing now.

JD

It's quite strange for a material like stone to be carved or detailed in some way to make it seem visually lighter.

AB

Well I think there are questions about functionalism and honesty in this project too. I don't really believe in honesty in architecture, I think illusion is much more interesting - the Baroque architects had it right.

JD

So here you are creating an illusion through a pavilion that is made of stone, but which folds down and across itself in a manner unexpected in masonry.

AB

Yes, and purists would say 'oh my god, you're not doing these things in the way stone should be done' - like stacking it, or making it thinner at the top - but you don't have to do that any more. Modern technologies mean we can do pretty much what we want, but we try to do it within reason and a strong conceptual basis.

An example is our new project in Folkestone. The competition brief asked for a multi-purpose 250 seat thea-

tre, but we also approached it as an urban response to the site. Even at the competition stage we proposed a whole series of improvements to Tontine Street, a really run down and neglected former main street of Folkestone, by making it a boulevard with trees and connecting it to the nearby harbour. We immediately took the approach that this building should form a continuation of the existing streetscape, something that reinforces its consistency. At the same time we proposed a new public square which acts as a forecourt to the theatre. The jurors told us that we were the only one of the presenting practices that talked about the urban context - everybody else just showed a building.

It has a very simple foyer at the ground floor, and a level entrance into the theatre. I suppose the main gesture is the really lofty first floor bar and restaurant, which we described as the 'living room' of Folkestone. It could also be used as a café and restaurant outside of theatre operating hours. It has that piano nobile quality of lifting you off the rubbishy level of the street. You have a great vantage point from there right down to the sea, and also looking out over the square.

This project has a very low budget, so we had to think realistically about how we were going to create a really efficient box - and then how could we give that box life and animate it. After a lot of research we were compelled to reference the oceanic iconography that you find right now in Folkestone - a lot of the buildings on Tontine Street have scallop shell architraves, and there are scallop trinkets in the local tourist shops.

JD

So the façade mimics those scallop shells?

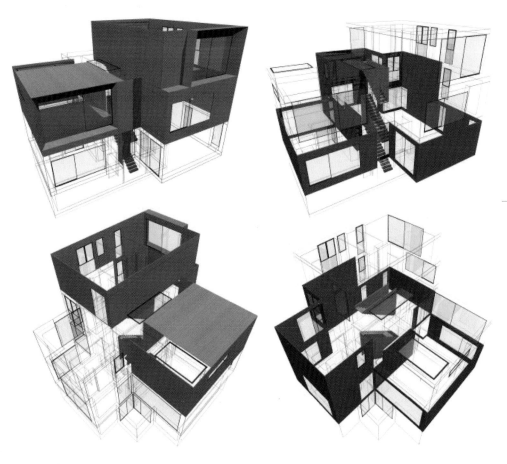

Studies of houses

Theatre in Folkstone

AB

Well the original idea for the cladding was that it
would be polycarbonate turned vertically and then
compressed so that it would bulge out - the whole
façade would be read as shell-like or fluted. But at a
very early stage we had to change the cladding to expanded metal mesh because polycarbonate is much
too fragile, too lightweight - it would just get destroyed.
Actually, we really wanted to use an opalescent acrylic
- but not only does it scratch, it's also not got a fire
rating - it can't be used as an exterior cladding material. So instead we came up with the proposition of
using expanded metal mesh, which I've used before
with Ron Arad in our One Off Studio when we made
our shell roof membrane out of compressed sheets of
it. What's interesting about this project is that we've
turned the orientation of the mesh so that it emphasises the curvature of the bulge - because the cuts
are vertical, when you look at it from one side it's solid,
while from the other side it looks open.

We also spent a lot of time thinking about the context and the harbour and the great light that comes
from the sea - they all make up a kind of 'conventional'
technicolour seaside experience. This will be that sort
of theatreland building - it will be illuminated and animated at night by lights behind the panels. It'll look like
lace - but actually it's a tough material like walkway
grating. The most economical way we can do this is
to project light from floodlights at the top and bottom,
but if more budget comes in we would use LEDs and
have the whole thing evenly lit. That way it could be
programmed by visiting artists, and have a whole colour scheme in LEDs. Depending on who was commissioned to do the light installation it could, say, slightly
pulse or change colour across its length.

In a way I think coming in as an outsider I'm more prone to see the potential in things that others are too familiar with. When ABA first went to Folkestone I thought it was the greatest place - this undiscovered gem on the South coast of England. I thought, 'why isn't everyone coming here?' It has a fish market and this quite authentic harbour which hasn't been destroyed by games arcades, and it's a bit run down but it has some really nice shops. I thought 'this is great', and it was only afterwards that I found out it has the highest crime rate in the whole South East - it's a really troubled place.

JD

It's good to be able to approach a project with 'new eyes' in a sense, and not be burdened by any preconceptions.

AB

Yes, exactly. On a recent site visit we went into Saint George's cathedral in Liverpool - and although it looks ominous and melancholy from outside, it's amazing inside. The stained glass does incredible things to the light inside that massive building. But I don't think many architect's would even bother to go in - they probably went on a school trip when they were twelve, and they wouldn't bother to go again - whereas I went just as another 'pupil'.

JD

I'm not really surprised that you enjoyed that building - a lot of your work involves creating dramatic voids and lightwells. You seem to intentionally break buildings down so that light gets into what would be the depths of a building, making them feel as connected to the outside as any other point. Producing enclosure without creating isolation too.

Mock-up of cladding for Theatre in Folkstone

AB

It's true - a journalist who went to see the Salt House said it was very porous, and I agree with that - we try to make all our architecture very porous. It is a light-handed way of sheltering or separating people from the exterior, while making you always feel quite closely connected to the outside. It means that at the very heart where you expect things to be most solid, it's most open – an inversion of the way houses are conventionally arranged.

alison brooks architects
ash sakula architects
dRMM
dsdha
mangera yvars architects
niall mclaughlin architects
youmeheshe

Recent projects.
An interview with Cany Ash
of Ash Sakula Architects.

CA -   Cany Ash
JD -   Jeg Dudley

JD

The housing you produced for the Peabody Housing Association in East London is located in an area undergoing huge development at the moment. What were your first impressions of the site and its surroundings?

CA

The site is situated in the once gated Silvertown yards part of the former London docks, a strip of land between the Thames and the Royal Docks. To the north on the Royal Docks are new quarters of dockyard-inspired flats, which have maritime features fronted by young fruit trees, and punctuated by cranes preserved as landscape features. Immediately to the south are tight terraces of nineteenth century dockers housing. While we were designing our four flats a new area called 'Silvertown Quays' was being planned on the wasteland between our site and City Airport with huge housing developments, a massive aquarium and a few schools.

While we were constructing our flats, a new Docklands Light Railway line was being built section by section, and I got a sense of what it might have been like to live in Victorian London when it was in rapid transition. You can feel the last remnants of a certain period of history being wiped out and a new world taking its place – this is apparent with the new university buildings and Thames Barrier Park, and the thriving economy that is driving the Excel Exhibition Centre on the other side of the Royal Docks.

Our site is a little sliver of land where older yellow stock brick houses meet red brick 1980's Peabody houses. Somehow the compression forced by the roads, river and docks throw up surreal contrasts. The backdrop is picturesque a look out tower from WW2 and other artfully scattered industrial remnants in a wasteland with lots of sky cut by low flying planes. We were very aware that this was a kind of cartoon strip 'frontier' land to the Thames Gateway – so in that context it felt right to make some, albeit quite small, landmarks which might have some influence on future building.

At the start of the design process we looked at what we thought was the main thing wrong with both council housing and with low cost housing generally. There isn't any space given to those key moments when you are meeting and greeting somebody or saying goodbye. In most houses you open the door onto a dark corridor and before you can actually talk to anyone,

View of entrance to housing units

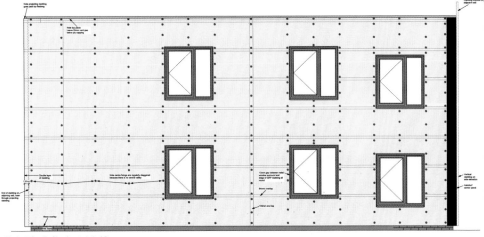

Typical detail of horizontal cladding

they have to follow you along the corridor before you can turn around. It just doesn't work especially when there is a lot of people filing through. Instead, we talked about the main hallway being a luminous room in its own right and a 'sorting' zone. The picture we did for the competition which was a mock working drawing, instead of 'technical' notes there were experiential notes- the pragmatic and poetic elements you need in a home and activities like pairing socks and paying bills.

JD

It's a space that would traditionally be considered useful for circulation only - but you've expanded it and carved out an unexpected additional space. In fact you've done something similar with the external entrance deck too.

CA

The external access is managed like a tree with decks that can be staggered to create space in front of each flat. This kind of inward facing outdoor space provides quite a lot of privacy but also quite a lot of community. That is something that has worked, even though we've built only four houses. We wanted people to enjoy conversation with their neighbours while sitting out and gardening. Thresholds spaces need to be more generous so that you can make them more your own. They were to have gates and small sheds, over time I think they will become quite customised spaces. The occupants have got into deck and garden breakfasts in the summer.

JD

And what were the intentions behind the most unusual aspect of these flats - the facades?

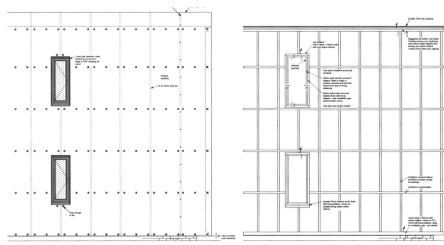

Typical detail of vertical cladding

CA

Do you know a book called Lightness by Ed van Hinte and Adriaan Beukers? I liked a lot of the ways he talked about economy of means and low embodied. So when this competition came up we thought about how we could make the construction very lean - timber cassettes that get clothed in something light and effective like a raincoat. Silvertown made us think this should be a glamorous raincoat like a Perspex and chrome make up case or well presented sandwich. We wanted this 'Quality Street wrapper' effect. That way it was not simply a light weight facade you would be able to see and feel that lightness.

The most robust transparent material is GRP as used on oil rigs and riot police shields. We tried to find manufacturers in the UK for the GRP, but they all made quite murky GRP which is fine if it is only seen

against the sky as a roof light in an industrial shed. We found that it is in fact more of a recipe than a material or product. There are many recipes. People chop the fibres at different lengths and add different amounts of phenolic resin. The look of the material can be very different: either it looks like Japanese rice-paper screens, or it can look muddy and more earthy. We went out to factories and saw how it was made.

GRP is again a live issue for us at the moment. Right now we're working on a Maynard's toffee factory in Newcastle which was burnt down in an arson attack - the roof fell in and it's more or less gone. We want to stitch it back together and add another couple of storeys to it in order to create a cluster of studios and allow it to be seen from further afield. The obvious thing to use is glass but glass isn't transparent in a way and it's not always reflective in the right way either - it can

View of entrance to housing unit

be quite gloomy and heavy looking. Instead we're playing with objects that should look like teeth or toffees or embedded into the brick factory.

So at the moment we're thinking what to make them out of and deciding whether fibreglass is a suitable technology. Atelier Van Lieshout, the one who wrote a book called The Good, The Bad and The Ugly a few years ago, used GRP for some toilets in Rotterdam in an interesting way. In places the material is barely translucent, and then it becomes almost transparent, and then it shifts back again. That's the kind of freedom you have when building something up in layers. You can make an extremely glossy exterior but quite a rough glass fibre interior. We're considering that approach for the Maynard's factory project.

JD

Did you consider any materials other than glass reinforced plastic for the Silvertown flats?

CA

For the two flat front facades we originally intended to use lapped natural Eternit panels as a contrast to the silver wrap, But in the end we used GRP and differentiated it from the back façade by using a smaller gauge, aligning the GRP horizontally not vertically. We were looking for a lightweight solution which would be simple and sustainable to transport and build so it was good to omit one material. The two different gauges worked well together one was a flexible material which could wrap around the curved rear facade of the building like a curtain and the other mimicked the brickwork in adjacent houses and was easily broken with windows. GRP was available, inexpensive, durable and beautiful - so we used it.

I think our Peabody housing is comic in a good way- the

upholstered look of the real rainscreen the silver foil takes the piss out of earnest industrial GRP and its fixings. The construction uses interior technology the foil is staple-gunned to the frame in the way you would re-cover a sofa. On the street you are very aware of this frame underneath - it's not pretending to be perfect.

I suppose this kind of façade construction is also a way of accepting the fact that architecture isn't a permanent thing; somebody might want to change the facade for something completely different. They can just unscrew it, and the frame will still be there, along with the breathable space and board - they can give it a new dress or a new look. Actually I think that facades aren't finished when you leave site. Trendy developers write clauses in leases to stop net curtains and satellite dishes and any other suggestion that people might want to change the look of a building's 'perfect exterior'. It's particularly bad when buildings come down to the ground and there's this little tray of pea-shingle that says 'we're coming down now' - there's going to be nothing unexpected about this. What I mean is maybe architects could be less military when it comes to holding back landscape from buildings.

We wanted a soft junction between the ground and these flats. When we were doing the competition we wanted to grow things up behind the vertical sections of cladding - almost like a compressed greenhouse. The curling tendrils of electrical cable in Vinita Khanna Hassard art work was a response to this.

JD

There would have been a nice parallel between this blurred edge at the base, and the top of the building where you've 'blurred' the GRP - extending it above the roof line.

View of entrance to housing units

CA

We wanted to avoid capping the buildings. To stop vertical rain at the top of a rainscreen you see heavy aluminium sheets bent and lapped which always looks so final and definite. Instead we wanted the cladding here to dematerialise to a degree and have allowed the vertical rain to run between the two layers in the cladding.

There's a different, quite interesting effect when it's windy: the whole thing moves behind the GRP – the Apollo foil which is only staple-gunned to the frame wobbles, and the Fibralex GRP sheet wobbles, and then the wires move. There's also this incredible sense of movement as you walk past and the sun shines on it - if you walk past in an orange jumper it picks that up! This relates to that idea of impermanence - it does feel more kinetic - not just because the foil moves, also because the light plays games with it and exaggerates the effect.

It remains to be seen what will happen to the look of the exterior in the future. The GRP, which is slightly pre-yellowed, will also go darker over time. But none of this bothers us – it's quite interesting that the GRP starts to approach the colour of the foil. Because the sun hits the foil and then bounces back to the GRP, you get this double ageing effect in the colours - but it doesn't affect the structure at all.

It was quite a mad job taking the full size sample panels all the way down to Swindon for Zurich, the insurers, to look at. Because these dwellings were going to be sold on shared ownership mortgages - we had to have a 30 year lifespan guarantee for the façade system from them. Initially they seemed quite dubious about it but we had some good researchers supporting us at the BRE and we let them play with the materials; the foil is impossible to tear and the GRP very difficult to scratch. The Apollo foil material is used a

lot in the Middle East now - for temporary buildings. It's quite amazing stuff - if you want to you can order it needle so that it is vapour permeable.

Maybe I could show you some of the work we did on the Leicester Creative Business Depot? It's interesting because, unlike the Peabody housing, we had to deal with an existing building and this heavily influenced the design we settled on. The building - which was originally used as a bus depot - had a heavy concrete frame and was quite over structured, this meant we could cut a series of holes in it to open up certain spaces without worrying about what we cut out. However, this frame was not going to be very good at keeping heat in, so we overclad the front of the building in red brick, which made everybody very happy, and at the back we used Schuco cladding which was a reference to glazed courtyards in industrial areas - it's in an old rag trade area. In fact we clad both the existing building and the new building in the same way, with brick on the front and Schuco on the back.

JD

What was the reasoning behind the un-regimented arrangement of this glazed rear façade?

CA

Well we had to keep certain verticals running down the façade, otherwise the cost became too high, but we didn't want it to dominate - we were aiming for a heterogeneous facade that expressed the creativity going on inside, and to differentiate between studios. The building is for a network of growing businesses, so I think the joy of this composition is that someone working there can point up and say, 'I'm the second window along'. As part of this idea of every business having their own identity, we also thought that various casements panels would act as branding surfaces and allow tenants a place to project their projects rather than feel systematised by the façade.

There were stringent technical limitations on what the curtain walling system we had chosen could do structurally. Also we could not have unlimited transparent panels for reasons of heat loss, and the types of glass needed to provide protection against solar gain. We experimented with different panel arrangements in an iterative process - each time building physical models to examine the patterns created in the façade - this allowed us to finalise the arrangement. It is a building that know how to transform itself seen at a steeper angles the whole wall seems to turn from silver to gold - you see not only the gold box that is the meeting room at the top, but the gold pressure caps that protrude from the façade between studios.

JD

I take it that part of this experimentation included accurately analysing the solar gain passing through each of these façade alternatives?

CA

Yes - during the project the building was thermally modelled to work out the actual temperatures that were likely to be achieved in the offices. Some rooms were overheating in the afternoon quite badly, but with cross ventilation and the ability to pin point the actual temperatures and risks of occurrence, we could share our thinking with the clients at this stage in the design and solve the problem. In the end it was quite a cheap 'intelligent' building - all the windows open up at high levels so that the rooms are completely naturally ventilated.

The final façade is comprised of three different panel types. The first is a clear glass double glazed unit that is transparent. The second unit is also double glazed, but has foamed acrylic inserted between the two sheets of glass in order to diffuse incoming light. These panels retain heat well but are highly translucent and admit quite a lot of solar gain. The last panel has a varying amount of layers of lacy fibreglass matting inserted either side of the foamed acrylic - this creates varying opacities and reflects more solar heat gain. In some cases these panels incorporated further acrylic panels which were decorated with silkscreen prints by the artist Linda Schwab. Originally we did lots of tests with some printers in Germany who were going to use fade-resistant inks to bubble-jet print directly onto the fibreglass matting. The samples were beautiful but sadly they decided in the end not to risk rolling shards of glass through their giant printers!

JD

It sounds like the manufacturers on both of these projects took a keen interest in helping you develop particular materials - such as the specific mix for the GRP, or this composite artwork-cladding panel.

CA

All the suppliers were heavily involved - particularly for the Apollo Foil and Fibralex GRP at Silvertown, where the application of the product was not the usual. They helped us collect evidence and reinterpret the tests that had been done for different purposes. We had to investigate fire, wear and tear, the effects of UV and the passage of moisture in order to convince building control and Zurich Insurance that this was a serious kind of building technology. Whenever we can we bring the actual manufacturers in as early as possible to help inform the design. This is not always possible, but it's always useful. Basically it's research and development.

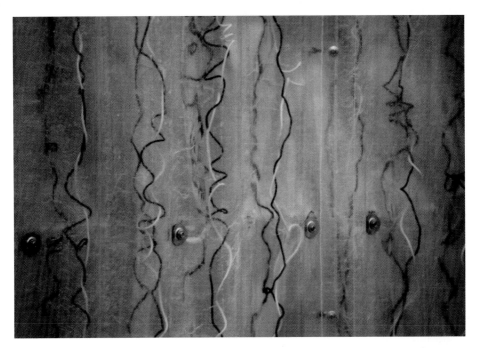

Views of cladding construction on site

Facades of Recent Projects.
An interview with Philip Marsh of dRMM

PM -   Philip Marsh
JD -   Jeg Dudley

JD

After the success of earlier projects where the envelope played a significant role in the architecture, how did you develop your approach to the design of the School in Clapham?

PM

Clapham Manor is a very successful Victorian Board school and part of the 'Beacon Schools programme'. Unfortunately it has been a victim of its success - it was designed as a one form entry school, but has grown and grown and is now a two form entry school in a one form entry building. This does mean though that Lambeth Council can apply for basic needs funding so that we can extend the school and provide the site with teaching accommodation that matches their growing requirements.

We spent about six months working with the school and the community, looking at different options for how we can develop the site. Actually, the context is really interesting - the Victorian Board school is only three storeys, but equivalent to a modern six storey building. Then there's the Oddfellows Hall and a row of terraces which are very early nineteenth century. In between these two exemplary examples of Victo-

rian (or slightly earlier) architecture is the space we eventually selected. It's the most awkward to develop, but for the school it was the only option because they don't lose any external play area and they keep the school under one roof (the reason they are successful, the school feels).

After that we looked at different articulations for the building. By pulling it away from the existing school we created a formal entrance, a glass link that separates the new from the Victorian. It has ended up sitting almost parallel with the Oddfellows Hall (a Grade II listed building), achieving a considered relationship with both nineteenth century buildings.

The last thing we wanted to do is a pastiche. Although the site is in a conservation area and the architecture of the old school and the Oddfellows Hall is beautifully proportioned and very considered, we felt it was important that we didn't try and find any relationship with the adjoining buildings' façades. Happily the Conservation Planner was open to contemporary solutions too. So we have developed this glazed façade that is almost random in its arrangement and avoids all these issues of composition. Having worked on Kingsdale School, I was very inspired by sixties school architecture and

Montage of proposed facade (for planning)

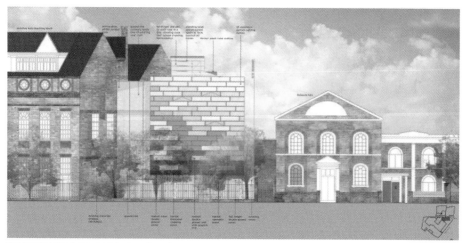

East Elevation: planning proposal showing colour scheme

the large areas of glazing. In particular, where the main building at Kingsdale turns a corner you get these fantastic glazed corners and nicely proportioned spaces. Here was an opportunity to reconsider the curtain wall approach, but use current technology to enhance it. So we've taken a Schüco curtain walling system and subverted it. While every example of curtain walling has a very regimented grid expressed on the outside, our cladding uses a concealed grid that means we are free to have the panels drift across the whole façade.

Since the windows aren't in a formal grid we developed a façade system that was loose enough to allow windows, insulated panels or fritted panels wherever we wanted them. Having developed these three types of panel that could be placed according to the environmental conditions, we worked with Fulcrum Consulting to look at their placement - for example, there are more insulation panels to the South where you get overheating.

JD

So is this project concerned with undermining the expected legibility of the building - stopping visitors from easily appreciating the functions of the rooms we are seeing into?

PM

Actually, for the Conservation Officer it was a problem that he couldn't determine the scale of the building without reference points. You get some solid banding that shows where the floors were - in those areas they had to have insulated or coloured panels. In a way all this does is put it more at odds with the Victorian building next door - that one is six storey high but only

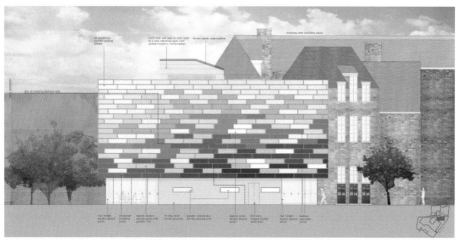

North Elevation: planning proposal showing colour scheme

has three storeys in it, while this building is not quite as tall but has four storeys. Fortunately, you don't get these bands running between the two buildings.

My education was initially interior design and then architecture so I am as interested in interiors, and a lot of the drivers for this project stemmed from the quality of the interiors of the classrooms. In the corridors at Kingsdale school we used a lot of linear visual windows, which are placed at different heights - some at floor level, some at high level - and those were one of the real successes of the remodelling of the original building. The school would have had more, had there been the money for them, as they really affected the children's behaviour and the feeling of transparency. These facades are informed by that idea too - you get these oblique, low level views which are especially suited to young children. Rather than having to peer over a window ledge, they can just look down from where they sit and see obliquely down to the street, and there are other views up to the sky.

However, when you go to schools and there are acres of glass you find that the teachers want to put things on the windows - so we made it possible here that all the solid panels are pinboards and things can be pinned to the windows, and they're acoustic absorbers as well.

It's great to exploit all the years of development in curtain walling technology and rely on that to create a fantastic watertight envelope, but then be a bit more playful with it because they are usually so restricted by a grid and are always associated with office blocks.

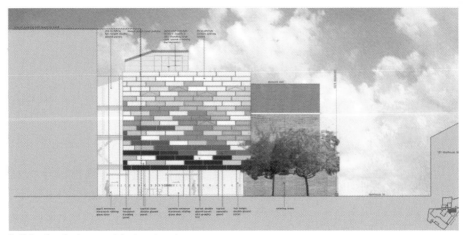
South Elevation: planning proposal showing colour scheme

JD

If you had a larger budget, would you have done more with the façade - like projecting out sections of it in order to make seating areas for the children, or larger windows in places?

PM

Actually, I wanted to keep the façade very smooth, and the windows are purposely within solid panels so you don't know where they are unless they're open.

If there was more money on the project I would spend it applying things to the interior - rather than benches projecting out, I'd set them within the façade and create more opportunities for bookshelves and thing so that the whole façade provides the storage, as well as pin-up space and solar shading. It would just work harder and harder.

Also the aluminium that forms the structure of the curtain walling would ideally, had money not been a restriction as it is on all educational projects, have been timber instead - a timber structure on the interior, and then glazed on the outside.

JD

The most striking element of this project has to be the vibrant range of colours across the facades - what was the thinking behind this?

PM

Well the building's colour scheme developed over a lot of iterations - we drew up some initial ideas that picked up on the contextual colours and also an idea that as you go around to the back of the school there's a surprise: you think you're going to see more of the same, but by then it's turned into a green building be-

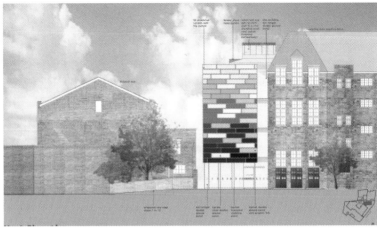

West Elevation: planning proposal showing colour scheme

cause it's referencing the soft landscaping and trees adjacent.

I was looking at glass technology and one manufacturer I visited was very proud of a new bubble jet printer they had just bought which could print any colour imaginable onto glass. They had a sample panel which was a piece of glass printed with all the colours you could want. In a way that was the inspiration for the colour treatment of the façade - take the whole range of colours and apply them to a building. So the colours shift from the reds and the yellows at the front of the Victorian board school and Oddfellows Hall, then as you go round a side alley they change through greens into blue at the back.

The other thing we did is to try to blend the richer hues at the level of the glazed plinth up into a white, allowing the building to dematerialise into the sky.

JD

That is a technique you're previously used on One Centaur Street, isn't it? On that project the spacing between the cladding panels increases as you move vertically up the building, making it melt into the skyline. On that project it's also aided by the aluminium wrapped insulation behind the cladding, which is a much lighter colour and becomes steadily more visible.

PM

Well it wasn't a conscious link between one and the other, but it's the same sort of thinking. On One Centaur Street that idea has worked to good effect - the building disappears up to the sky and there are very solid panels at the lower levels. On that project the panels are just a decorative screen - the aluminium insulated layer behind is doing all the work and is the real rainscreen. That allowed us to be playful with the outer cladding.

I think it's important to have a playful façade for Clapham Manor School too, but we don't want to patronise the pupils in any way. I suppose colour is the one thing that is very subjective. People can be quite alarmed by certain colours or shades - so I suppose if you provide a building with every shade then they are bound to find something they like!

JD

Perhaps we could move onto another educational project you've completed - the main building at Kingsdale school - which features a very large variable-skin ETFE roof. Could you explain how you chose that material during the design process?

PM

Following a series of workshops with the school community, we evolved a proposal to work with the existing building. One of the big moves was to demolish the existing hall that subdivided the two quadrangles in the school, and then realise one large space as a useable covered courtyard. Our initial design didn't use ETFE - we looked at using large timber members that spanned all the way across, and admitting very controlled north light. But obviously there would have been a downside in their weight, and we would have to have put elaborate columns in to support them. Instead, our engineer, Mike Hadi, introduced us to ETFE, which has the advantage of being very lightweight. So, we arrived at a very simple arch system supported by the existing 1950's structure.

JD

Did you work through lots of different options for the patterning of the ETFE?

PM

Vector, the ETFE cushion suppliers, had completed earlier examples of variable skin roofs before but they were quite simple in terms of the frit they developed - they just had a simple rectangular pattern that they alternated. But we saw this as a wonderful opportunity to create a fantastic op art pattern - in a way it's the largest op art piece in the world! We ideally wanted something that had a movement to it so that you could see rotations happening in the pattern, but we didn't want it so frenzied that the pupils became disorientated. Ultimately we erected on site a series of samples that Vector produced, and the headteacher, staff and pupils went out and selected what was for them a preferred pattern. There was also a specific requirement by Fulcrum Consulting for the roof to limit light transmission to between 5% and 55%.

The roof is actually in two parts - the main trusses that span the central space are cushions of variable skin ETFE with 3 layers, whilst around the perimeter there's a clerestory of clear ETFE which is the same as they've used at the Eden Project. At the short ends of the school Vector developed large vents that could open to draw fresh air in from ground floor level. This rises through the stack effect and discharges at either end. It's a tempered space, so it's unheated and is never quite as warm as the rest of the school, but in the depths of winter it's significantly warmer than outside. The roof traps the heat that dissipates through the leaky sixties façade, which, coupled with solar energy, provides a pleasant environment.

1:1 sample mock-up
(W 1000mm, H 800mm,
D 160mm)

1:1 sample mock-up
(W 1000mm, H 800mm,
D 160mm)

By covering the central space, it gives the school so many options - so much extra space to use for whole-school assemblies, dining, sport, exhibitions and as social space. We've also tackled the circulation that blighted the original Leslie Martin design. Moving all the circulation into the new space creates passive surveillance where everyone can see and be seen, and at its heart is the central auditorium.

The central auditorium didn't start out as a geodesic structure. We had a limited amount of money, but we knew we wanted something fantastic in the middle of this space, so we looked through a series of economic solutions. We looked at panel systems, sprayed concrete and finally at the work of Gordon Cowley. Gordon was the only viable option. We were able to exploit his years of experience with large timber structures, and using the principle of geodesics we could create a very

large envelope very economically. By using timber in the round - larch poles connected with steel and aluminium nodal joints - to form the structural gird faced in birch plywood from a local timber yard we created this fantastic thing which is also quite utilitarian in a way. The original Leslie Martin building suggested that it should be made of birch ply: on the second floor a small tiered lecture room had been built from wonderful bent birch plywood seats and desks, which informed the materiality of the auditorium.

JD

You experimented with timber construction in other ways on the Kingsdale Sports Hall. In that building you've taken KLH - a cross-laminated timber system - but then you pushed it a little, moving it away from simple rectilinear forms and producing instead the swooping, curved form of the roof.

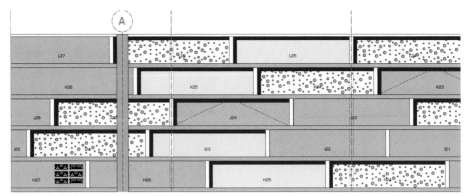

Detail internal elevation: typical classroom

PM

Certainly the most interesting element of the building is the articulated roof - just by taking a flat panel system and changing the frame height we created this incredible warped roof. You get a fantastic spatial experience inside.

I suppose traditionally, school sports buildings tend to be dumb metal boxes. But if you go to KLH in Austria and see their factory buildings you can see the possibilities for glulam columns and KLH wall panels. In fact KLH and Merk do these great cross-laminated systems where you can make each panel as big as you can transport, so it is perfect for large envelopes. We are just exploiting what the system does best.

JD

Your Naked House project followed similar lines.

PM

Again, we were just exploiting the benefits of a panel system and CNC technology. With Naked House, there is a direct relationship between computer-based design and the manufacturer, whose CNC automated cutting system allows freedom of form. The playful windows of the Music School at Kingsdale School are a direct expression of this: you can make windows and doors in any shape you like, as they are cut out by CNC at the factory.

JD

So there are two different but complimentary threads running through your work. One focuses on extreme customisation - the ability to offer whatever a single person or group wants - while the other uses prefabricated and standardised components, which you ensure are just as suited to their projects through careful detailing.

PM

It's very exciting to take standard products and tweak them to create a whole new palette of possibilities.

Internal view of typical classroom

The façade of our Wansey Street Housing uses a very utilitarian material - an Eternit fibre-cement board - which is then embossed with a timber grain. But by the application of colour and careful design, we are able to create this very bold façade, almost like a huge art piece, that blends from the yellows of the Victorian buildings to the terracotta of the town hall. So we've taken a plain material which is usually white in colonial houses and unarticulated and made it something quite special.

JD

And this brings up a theme present in much of your work - you seem to play games with people's expectations. In that project the fibre-cement board is given a timber grain and texture, but it's not wood. While for the Moshi Moshi restaurant project in Brighton you used a material than resembles traditional ricepaper screens, but is actually a GRP composite panel.

PM

Yes - Kalwall, an American translucent panel product.

JD

So you are playing a game where the automatic connections we make with materials are unexpectedly undermined when we examine them further and realize they are something else.

PM

Well, I think there are two approaches here. Sometimes, like with the Moshi Moshi example, there's a material we were conscious of but were waiting for the right application. Other materials like ETFE we didn't know about, but which then revealed themselves as the only solution. In the Moshi Moshi project it worked superbly. The formal grid that it creates is perfect within the context of a sushi restaurant.

Facades of Recent Projects.
An interview with Deborah Saunt of DSDHA

DS -   Deborah Saunt
JD -   Jeg Dudley

JD

How is work progressing on new projects?

DS

One project we are working on at the moment is for is a school in Dagenham.

It faces Dagenham Civic Centre which is very robust, so the outside facade is very civic, scale-less, while on the other side of the building has a courtyard in the middle and these beautiful canopied external areas which are almost like rooms.

It's decorated in patterns that we developed with the graphic artist Oliver Klimpel and the school children, through asking them what they enjoyed on their way to school. We thought, you know, it's Dagenham: Ford, cars, the A13 - they're going to talk about different vehicles, maybe infrastructure. Instead they talked about foxes, squirrels, rabbits - stuff we didn't even know was there, but the kids just see so differently.

It was fantastic. So we reconfigured this local fauna and developed the idea - we've used it as an exterior surface treatment to the spaces that the children occupy. It has been screen printed as a camouflage of animals that wraps the walls and illuminated canopies above. We have also used it on the windows as manifestation, and inside the spaces there are great big de-scaled animals to decorate the walls. Some of the staff are freaked out - but the kids love it! In a way we pull the rug out from under preconceptions of what things should be for adults and children.

We're also working on two new buildings in Potter's Field Park, next to GLA for MoreLondon. One of the two pavilions is in Blossom Square, and is made of white stained timber and glass - it's going to have an extensive grass roof so that it should look like an extension of the park when you look down from above – as you do from Tower Bridge and the GLA. That building has a budget a quarter of the other, so we couldn't push the boat out technically with the elevations and focused on the roof as the fifth elevation.

The other pavilion will have a burnt timber façade - right now we're conducting material tests in the joinery workshop looking at the junctions and the level of burning for the finished building. We've been testing various samples for the last two years- burning them with a blowtorch - to decide the duration of charring.

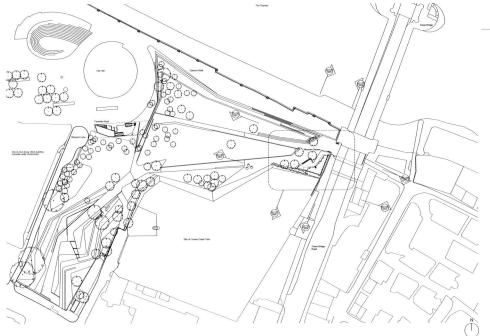

Site plan: Potter's Field Park

JD

Do you think the timbers will stay quite dark black, rather than fade to lighter greys over time?

DS

Yes, that's our expectation. Based on what we know now, absolutely. If you go to the Australian bush where there's been a bush fire, the trees are still charred many, many years after. Charring has this amazing resistance to rot and weathering - it gives you that protection. In fact, only very recently did we discover about the ancient Japanese technique called Yakisugi where timber is burnt for construction ...

One of the parameters we're testing here is about how far we can push innovation our client – after all this is a public building in a very prominent location, it's not a private institution where your can protect the building for investigation or exposure. So this burnt treatment was our preference, and in the end we liked it because you touch the material and some charcoal gets rubbed off as a trace – so the building becomes personal.

As a material, this option appealed to us because of its integrity; the way in which its grain reappears on the burnt surface, revealing a hidden quality that only appears when you burn it and then wash it down. What's ironic is that the one we chose is darker than the other options but is actually burnt less than the lighter finish - the others are all burnt twice and washed twice, and this version is burnt only once and washed once.

Behind all this material investigation is a narrative capturing the turmoil that's occurred on the site over time. For us it was inspired by the very first visit we made to the site when a taxi driver from Elephant and

Castle dropped us off and he told us Potters' Fields and MoreLondon used to be a bomb site there. We went to the records office and found bomb maps that showed this site was heavily hit during the Second World War. Of course you go there now and it's corporate and part of London as a global city. So the idea is that this building negotiates between that contemporary condition and the echoes of things that have happened on the site. It should also engage with that community of people who still remember the history of the site and will come to Potters' Fields Park as their park. We want to capture some of that resonance on site.

JD

The buildings are quite considerate - they seems to capture small pockets of that garden without detracting from the larger focuses like Tower Bridge, the Tower of London, the GLA, and so on. I remember reading an article in which you talked about not wanting the buildings to be imposing at all...

DS

I think they can do both - they can oscillate between being incredibly modest and intimate, and also being quite forthright.

I was there today and Gross Max's park is looking amazing, it's not open yet but it's just sublime. I was walking through this space thinking 'this is central London – fantastic!' And there are unexpected delights about the buildings too - the cantilever is designed to frame a view of Traitor's Gate on the river and this is a poignant statement about this particular location amongst all the glamour and urbanity. It's not a pretty tower or a pretty castle – it is a scary environment where political prisoners were once disposed of, but people tend to forget that – they and get caught up

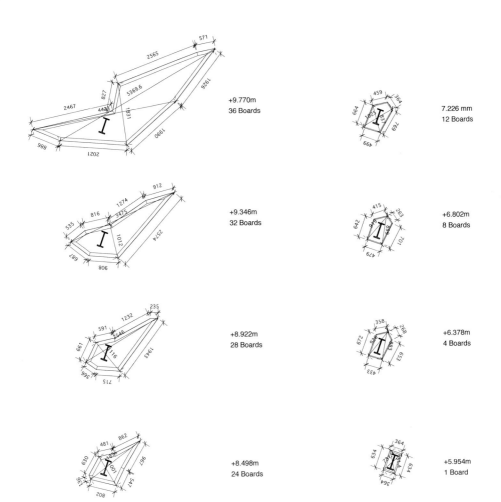

+9.770m
36 Boards

7.226 mm
12 Boards

+9.346m
32 Boards

+6.802m
8 Boards

+8.922m
28 Boards

+6.378m
4 Boards

+8.498m
24 Boards

+5.954m
1 Board

Parkside kiosk column and wall details

Blossom Square kiosk: working progress of timber samples

in today's concerns think of it as being this heritage landmark and not a real place where life took place.

It's also interesting in urban terms knowing more and more about the real history of places like the Tower of London and Westminster Abbey. Lots of these buildings up until the 19th Century used to be encrusted with other buildings, clinging on like limpets around their exterior. These additions were amazingly complex in geometry and structure grafted onto the Tower of London, the whole elevation was jostling with little buildings - and there was still Traitor's Gate beneath. The landmark was encrusted with all the busy-ness and messiness of a city. But along came a brutal brigade in the 1880's who just sanitised all our old public buildings. I just think it's so vital that we go back to remembering that stuff is messy and layered.

You spoke about the buildings having a background-ness, but the funny thing is, if you stand in another corner of the park and walk up the pathway past the new building Foster and Partners have just built, you get a diagonal view under the pavilion's canopy and it looks like Tower Bridge is being eaten by our building - which is great! There are poignant and aggressive views here - we like the idea of such an icon being eaten by a kiosk!

I suppose another aspect of our urban landscape work is that we are very interested in scale - scale as a design tool. Having worked a lot with children you discover that if you strip a building of any scaled references it can be what you want it to be, at any time of day or your life. You can think of it as imposing or intimate - or you can let it be between those things. We argue that because the minute you revert to those elements that have scale, you have to do it so consciously. It's a real challenge and you make construction much more difficult by removing those downpipes and other standard things. But I think that's what makes it great architecture and not just building.

JD

I think that's apparent in Paradise Park's vegetated façade, which is intriguing because there is no 'standard scale' to refer to for such an element - it's some-

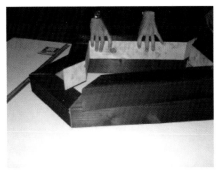

Blossom Square kiosk: working progress of timber samples

thing you just don't usually see.

DS

Well it's almost vertiginous - the first time I ever saw a vertical garden in Paris my brain just didn't know how to locate it, because everything you've ever been told is that plants grow up from the horizon. It was in Hotel Pershing Hall, by Andree Putman, a luxury hotel near the Champs Elysees. It was terrific.

JD

And is that a thick, matted vegetated wall? Because the most noticeable feature of the Paradise Park wall is that it isn't a thick matrix - and it doesn't really attempt to be - it is quite honest in showing the greenery as sporadic over the surface.

DS

Yes, Paradise Park isn't as dense!

JD

This seems to reflect a theme in your work - a relaxed attitude to the materials you use. It seems like DSDHA would never say 'if this is going to be a green wall, then it must be perfect and of a totally even density and cover'. Instead you are happy for elements to not be faultless, like the unevenly charred timbers we discussed earlier.

DS

Well it is not really about being relaxed! It is more of a critique. We think that sort of perfectionism gives architecture a bad name. It's not what life's like. Anybody who has built a project knows that the moment you finish it, it's dissolving and kind of crumbling. Buildings are always on the move and evolving - they are organisms as well as edifices. Life's too short to get upset about the notion of finality and the absolute. It is an obsessive western preoccupation. We only get really upset when our details are not followed or when services are not in the right place. So we're as controlling as we can be, but we're realists. I think it's a political statement - I don't think it's appropriate for architects to demand that degree of control over everything, because it's intimidating and it's not convivial.

I know that when we build we do demand 'the best'

View of Blossom Square kiosk from Tower Bridge

and this can mean that we make ourselves hugely unpopular.

At the end of the day, part of me would love it all to be perfect, but there's no such thing as a perfect building. The nearest thing I've been to a "perfect" building is the Prada store in Tokyo. That is a building without budget! I walked in and, to be absolutely honestly, within two minutes I said 'I don't think I can be an architect anymore' - it was absolutely extraordinary. I walked up, around the building, came back down – and then just at the very last moment as I came down the back stair I saw a flange of metal sticking out that was definitely not meant to be there. I was so relieved!

JD

And do you think your own use of materials has evolved in your projects?

DS

Yes it has certainly evolved. Our early work really was about learning to apply a façade - we were dealing with pavilions and that's one of the simple manoeuvres you apply to them. You've got a limited budget, limited technical capacity as a small practice and you are learning how far you can go with clients - so you necessarily confine your enquiry to one element. But also it terms of the architectural logic, having a façade that is legible and separate is fine. Whereas now, because we are increasing in our sophistication and complexity and confidence, we can look at slicing buildings and manipulating them in a more ambitious way that grows with the complexity of the programmes and uses that we are given to work with.

JD

It also seems like you have moved on from just taking standard materials and using them in inventive ways,

into actually producing your own: the screen printed aluminium panels for the school in Dagenham, and the burnt wood façades for the Potter's Field Park project.

DS

I think having more confidence has meant that we can work with our clients to make these bespoke materials which fascinate us, but we still like using ready-made things. We do worry that we might be considered a little bit indulgent in that insistence on always using something that is new. Take the aluminium cladding in the William Bellamy School in Dagenham - that is bespoke, not a standard aluminium product. We think we shouldn't lose our connection with the ready-made product and should keep that point of enquiry, because it's a criticism levelled at architects as they increase in stature - that they can end up using materials on a whim.

That's why perhaps we have insisted on using brick in a new school project in Guildford - there was an odd discussion amongst the team at the start about what this building should be made of. We just felt brick deserved our attention - this material that is so maligned and that the carpeted 1920's estates of northern Guildford are made of, why should we not try to embrace it and see what can be done with it?

We've used it before on the John Perry School in Dagenham in a certain way, so it was now a case of 'how can we use it again without repeating that solution?' That for us is a strong rule. We try never to use the same material twice. But I actually wonder if that's appropriate or sustainable – for example brick is such a complex material maybe we should use it many times.

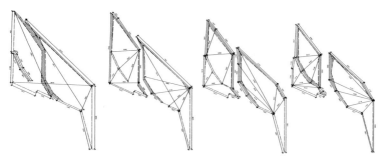

Parkside kiosk soffit details

JD

I imagine that this experimentation with materials also requires a high degree of collaboration - you have to feel confident when you design or select these unusual materials that the engineers or contractors or artists you work with will be on board.

DS

And the clients as well - the clients are amazing. We've done three buildings in Dagenham - two are in polycarbonate, and one in aluminium. The aluminium one is radical - it's only when you finish that you stand back and think, 'what a great client - who is happy to work hand in hand with architects who want to do something different'.

Here, the client knows it also means something in an area which is really desperately seeking new meaning at the moment - I don't know if you are aware of the BNP and Dagenham, but it is one of the most divided parts of London at the moment.

When we were on site last year, we stood outside the school and saw a racist situation happen right in front of us - I'd never seen that before. It is unnerving to make public architecture in a context where you have this happening. But we relate that back to the building's facade - architecture is an act of communication, and you know if you are communicating in this context the weight of that communication is different to one when working in a very metropolitan area, like Potters Field Park, where people have a sort of "world city" mentality. We have to choose our materials to specifically engage with the range of audience a particular to a project.

But when we design, this process of material investigation is not overtly conscious - I really have to emphasise that. It's not like we think 'right, we're going to produce this building that's schizophrenic or emotionally charged" - each project is a balance of what is hoped for and the real qualities that are revealed after the fact, and I suppose in this case we were trying to create something very robust, very firm and simultaneously delightful in this community in absolute flux. I mean real flux - the demographic shift in that area has

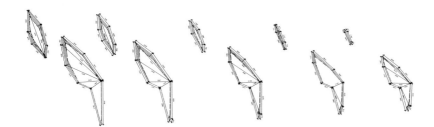

Parkside kiosk soffit details

been colossal. Total diversity across so many different communities - marginal communities from the centre of London are being relocating to the edge, to places like Dagenham, so the monoculture is shifting and there is a lot of readjustment within the communities.

JD

The John Perry buildings are very sensitive to their context in other ways - they refer to the industrial language of their surroundings, but subtly subvert it: they use slightly glossy, pixelated brickwork which is just beyond the norm, and large polycarbonate-panels for the inner wall facing the children's play area, which is also unexpected but very welcoming.

The building simultaneously defers to its surroundings quite strongly, while also making a bold statement to the people - or children - who use it. I can imagine as a child going into that building and feeling quite special, knowing that there is a side you see, but no one else walking past on the street knows about.

DS

Yes, that's a really nice way of thinking about it. I think we were very aware for all of those buildings, the ones in Dagenham and Manchester, that these are the first public buildings children experience and so you should try to inspire them by giving them something extraordinary. To try to relate to them as a sophisticated audience, as well as relating to the adults. It certainly affected me when I was young to have the privilege of going to beautiful buildings and of also being asked my opinion. I was in a public consultation when I was seven in Australia and was asked about my ideal notion of a classroom of the future - which I only realized many years later by talking to children and thinking, 'this feels really familiar' – that back then they asked me what architecture I would like.

For DSDHA as architects we talk about our work as a marriage of social innovation and technical innovation. We don't want to produce buildings that lie down and do not communicate, and that are just too polite.

Recent Projects. An interview with Ali Mangera and
Ada Yvars Bravo of Mangera Yvars

AM -   Ali Mangera
AYB   Ada Yvars Bravo
AW -   Andrew Watts

AW

What is the Abbey Mills Islamic Centre?

AYB

We have developed a concept for Abbey Mills Centre to build a markaz, or multifunctional mosque. A markaz is an international centre that aims to reach out to both the wider Muslim and non-Muslim community alike. The International Islamic Centre will aim provides prayer areas for men and women, a school, library, offices, residential areas and public space. One of the core principles of the Markaz is to help disadvantaged youth and the Markaz will provide dedicated youth facilities, including sports and recreation areas.

AW

The project uses an ambitious, and rather beautiful language of construction. How is Centre organised spatially?

AM

The project aims to create a mixed use environment based on the idea of a 'campus' rather than a single building. We have designed a mosque, a School, an Islamic Arts and Exhibition Space, big library and facilities for teenagers and children. These components will all be set into an Islamic garden. The site is significant, being about a kilometre long! So we want to capitalise on its visual impact by making the scheme link strongly to the 2012 Olympics, which is located nearby. We would like to see the project being used as an 'Islamic Quarter' for the Games, the benefits of which are already appreciated by the London Development Agency.

The site is very interesting in that the local area, the Lower Lea Valley, is an area undergoing enormous change at the moment. The local borough, Newham, has one of the most ethnically mixed communities in London, with a growing immigrant community. Half of the local population is of an ethnic minority origin, a quarter of which is Muslim. So this project is about finding a home for some that energy and transition in what will be Europe's largest mosque and Islamic centre.

AW

What is the site currently used for?

AYB

Abbey Mills is currently one of the most contaminated brownfield sites in the UK, The site was operated as

Aerial view of Abbey Mills Centre

the West Ham Chemical Works during both World Wars, but contamination has recently been capped. In order to reclaim the land for construction and bring some natural beauty back to the site, we have proposed a new Islamic Garden as the generating principle for the project. The Garden is essentially a space for contemplation, both in a religious sense and as a way of being able to appreciate the physical environment of this corner of South East England. When transposed onto modern day multi-ethnic London the garden will be like the city square, a place of refuge from the familiar pressures of urban life. The garden will contain courtyards, terraces and passages in a varied landscape. Our intention is to set an olive grove at the centre of the Garden as a symbol for peace. So I suppose we are creating a new London park.

While developing the design, we asked ourselves 'how can architecture represent faith?. Religious architecture which is heavily symbolic often becomes a parody of itself, making it somewhat meaningless. This is something we definitely want to avoid in our design: Sacred space should be manifestly symbolic. The symbolic repertoire associated with an Islamic architecture may include domes, minarets, calligraphy and geometric motifs. The starting point of our scheme however is to question our brief and our assumptions about what an Islamic architecture should be.

AW

So did you examine what the nature of a contemporary mosque might be?

AM

A mosque is governed by and can be reduced to the etiquette and rules of prayer. In Islam this is determined by the Quibla or direction of prayer to Mecca and lines of the congregation or 'Saf'. The mosque in its simplest form can therefore be seen as field represented by axis and direction. Our scheme is organized as a confluence of Quibla and Saf lines which flow across the site. In many ways we see the project as urban Islamic 'calligraphy'.

The confluence of landscapes, the movement induced by lines of saf and the varied geometry of the structure suggest that the project itself is a form of Islamic Calligraphy. Within this abstract and fluid matrix, by coincidence or otherwise the project can be seen to spell out Quranic verse. The direct use of calligraphy, as a decorative applied art will be used to bind the various programmatic elements from the school to the mosque. The Quran will be written on surfaces across the Markaz site, seamlessly linking the building and the program.

AW

How will the non-Muslim community be able to use the building?

AM

Dawat or 'invitation' is a key aspect of Islam. The scheme interprets the idea of invitation by providing an interstitial public space between the inner sanctum of the mosque and the world outside. The project physically and metaphorically reaches out to provide large urban connections inviting visitors into the building. Invitation space will be used as an outdoor public forum; a place where Muslims and Non-Muslims can meet and promote a greater understanding of the fundamental links of ideology, faith and our precious common humanity.

AYB

You mentioned having wider community facilities. How are these provided?

Black aluminium facade render

Copper facade render

Pearlescent aluminium facade render

The project will provide a boarding school for 500 students and separate youth facilities for up to 2000 disadvantaged children from the neighbourhood. The youth facilities include 10 indoor sports fields and suites of IT and computer rooms. A sort of giant internet café! We have also thought about how the land is used. We want to incorporate allotment gardens which will be used to provide food for the buildings occupants, as would have been the case in this area before its industrialisation. We hope that he garden allotments will help to regenerate and renew the contaminated site. Provision would be made for training in small scale agriculture and sustainability for young urban volunteers who otherwise have little or no access to the countryside.

AW

The multiple functions of the Islamic Centre suggest highly adaptable space. How are you achieving this in the design?

AM

The layout of the scheme avoids compartmentalising activity by setting up zones where building functions either merge or spill into one another. We want to encourage unexpected conversation between the mosque elders and younger users of the building in a campus-like environment in a way that is conducive to debate.

As the number of people using the centre fluctuate in different parts of the Centre, spaces can be extended or compressed in peak periods through the use of inflatable structures which temporarily cover outdoor areas. Although the language of the building is definitely one of permanence, or durability, the buildings will also adopt the language of nomadic structures or tented cities. The proposed structural system for the

buildings is formed by distorting traditional geometric Islamic patterns to form a fractal structural series. A sort of fractal space frame I suppose! A system of overlapping ribs will be used with the rib pattern providing a geometric decorative layer, which in turn supports the characteristic metallic cladding of the sweeping form of enclosure.

AW

So is the use of light as significant as the use of form in the project?

AM

The journey from the world outside into the world of the mosque is accentuated by the use of both light and sound. The form and position of the mosque roof and minarets allow reverberation and echo. Light is brought into the mosque in geometric patterns through openings in the lattice roof structure and cladding. In terms of accentuated lighting, the overall emphasis will be to illuminate the leading Quibla wall facing Mecca. The 'dome', or its equivalent as a dominating aspect of the roof form, will be clad in translucent panels. At night, when seen from afar, the building will appear to have an inner glow through a translucent skin.

AW

You mentioned a concern with the sustainability in the use of the land occupied by the project. Are there other aspects to this green – or brown – thinking?

AM

This area experiences significant winds from autumn to spring, which we would like to benefit from in the form of wind turbines in order to generate electricity. As a part of this, wind catchers to be used to eliminate the need for mechanical cooling. The site also benefits

Project in Middle East

from the tides in the Channelsea River next to the site. We have proposed that the river be dredged to allow us to generate additional electricity from tidal power.

AW

You are also working on a smaller scale Islamic Centre in South London. How is this project developing?

AM

The South London Islamic Centre wants to demolish its existing centre in Mitcham and build a set of purpose made buildings which support an ambitious range of activities for the local community. The new centre will provide dedicated prayer facilities for men and women, community halls, exhibition spaces, a dining facility and a small school. It is hoped also that the centre will also accommodate an indoor sports and recreation hall. The built area of the scheme could be between 4000 to 5000 square metres.

From my point of view, mosques and Islamic community centres in Britain have rarely been assessed in terms of their architectural intent, design quality and contribution to the wider cityscape. For a variety of reasons, the architecture of many British mosques is often a pastiche representation of historic Islamic architecture reduced to artificial domes and fake minarets. This type of architecture has little relevance to our cityscapes and has done much harm to the status and outward expression of the Muslim community in Britain today.

The project in Mitcham will be a contemporary expression of Islam relevant to the future aspirations of the Muslim community in the context of modern day multi-cultural Britain. We have some understanding Islamic architecture in its philosophical sense and we want to interpret these fundamental requirements in way which integrates itself with the cityscape and contributes to its development. The idea of the courtyard, the reverberation of the call to prayer, the use of water, light, pattern and geometry can be reinterpreted with a contemporary architectural expression and be made suitable for the needs of the South London Islamic Centre.

AW

How are you integrating the design with the site context?

AYB

The SLIC site is a former fire station. The building sits in a parade of shops with residential accommodation above. The site is bound on one side by The Church of the English Martyrs and the rear of the site backs onto residential gardens. The SLIC site is also in close proximity to St. Leonard's Church. We have made one of the core aims of the project to create spaces which are open to Muslims and Non Muslims alike. The new scheme will create a dialogue space as a garden or a

foyer which between The Church of the English Martyrs and the new SLIC building. This space will act as a physical and metaphorical bridge between faiths. The foyer of the SLIC will also be linked visually to Streatham Green in front SLIC centre.

Public Functions such as the cafeteria, restaurant and exhibition space will be set adjacent to the main entrance. We aim to attract a range of people into the building including those of the wider community who may normally not consider entering a mosque. The new building will create an integrated architectural response to the site with a single unified vision of the meeting of faiths. Like the Abbey Mills project, the SLIC scheme will use geometric Islamic patterns inscribed into building surfaces. Daylight will be filtered through the patterned surface of the building to create geometric shadows. The massing of the built volumes will benefit from solar heat gain and natural light in winter through the use of glazed winter gardens. The central courtyard could act as a dynamic space for solar gain in winter and cooling in summer.

AW

In another project on the rural edge of London, you are proposing an 'invisible' sports centre. Not much room for architectural expression then?

AM

The project is for a sports centre at Range Farm in Essex. Our approach to the site is rooted in the idea of the maintaining the strength and character of the natural landscape, both in physical and social terms. We are proposing a building that integrates itself strongly with the landscape, seeing the road infrastructure and new building as part of the landscape rather than separate objects, aiming to make as little visual or environmental impact as possible.

This approach has its origin in the land art practice of the 1960's, with Robert Smithson's work as the best known example. In later years, architects such as Oscar Niemeyer, Zaha Hadid and Foreign Office Architects have produced work that mediates the relation between buildings and landscapes. We have used the landscape to camouflage the building, thus minimising the visual impact it would have on the surroundings. The sports hall will be sunk down into the ground, permitting only two to three metres to extend above ground. Sloping ground planes will help conceal the building further, burying it in a discreetly undulating landscape.

Two options have been developed for the project, each with the same built volumes. One option is organised around a series of distinct cuts in the ground plane, tilting it up or down to generate openings and enclosures in the landscape. The building acts as a filter, with visitors entering on the west side of the building

and emerging out on the east side facing the sports fields. The roof of the building is constructed as a landscape terrace, allowing visitors to access and use the surface for play and sports. A second option is based on the idea of one continuous façade facing the sports field, and is similar to option 1 in being buried below ground. The layout is arranged around the curved façade, giving each sports activity a visual link to the outdoors sports field. The landscape will be divided into distinct territories or 'tectonic plates, each with its specific spatial characteristics. In both options, rooflights perforate the partially buried building, bringing daylight in to the sports hall, changing rooms and swimming pool.

The proposal aims to use local and recycled materials and resources as much as possible. The use of brown roofs is one of the ways we can utilise left-over materials from the site excavation and construction process. These materials can to an extent also be used for landscaping features, where the ground needs grading to accommodate sports pitches and sloping elements.

AW

Explain a little about your new project in Abu Dhabi.

AM

We recently won a major competition there to design ten residential towers, a hotel and large housing scheme in Abu Dhabi. We are excited about the scheme because we find the Middle East a fascinating place to be right now.

Cities in the Middle East are entering a new phase. In regions like the Gulf, the idea of the city is in flux. The idea of 'urban context' or 'landscape' as we would understand from a European city does not exist in the same way in the Gulf. This is both liberating and problematic. For us now, understanding the significance of Middle Eastern City- perhaps through the idea of new landscape morphologies is a challenge. Moreover we feel there is a certain political and ideological basis to our work – primarily our understanding of Muslim societies in the UK which enables us to act with confidence in dealing with cultural significance of working in the Middle East.

AW

Your approach to the Gellatly Road project in Lewisham is much smaller than the other projects, but certainly makes no attempt to camouflage itself.

AM

You will perhaps not be surprised to learn that this project is set within a conservation area. The site is formed by a narrow infill space currently occupied by a single story garage in a Lewisham conservation area.

The addition to a house is slotted between a local shop and an existing Victorian house. The addition to the house is 2.5 metres wide at its narrowest point on the street. In order to provide as much usable space as possible, the scheme is organized around a structural and service 'island' placed acting as the core for the house. The floor, walls and roof of the house are hung and cantilevered off the island eliminating the need for perimeter structure and freeing valuable internal space. The island also acts as a support for the stair and kitchen. The kitchen is wrapped and twisted around the stair as it rises up making efficient use of the space available for work surfaces. The house is laid out as a series of distinct 'territories' separated by a stepped 'landscape' and 'mixing zones' rather than by any formal enclosure such as walls or partitions. These territories include the kitchen, gallery, bathroom and bedrooms. So I suppose our ideas about territories and landscape from the large scale sports centre we have just discussed have found a parallel in a much smaller scale building.

The upper volume is cantilevered and clad in a highly reflective metallic skin. With the absence of any obvious structural support, the upper volume will appear as a 'cloud'-like space floating over the house. The faceted cladding will reflect the sky, providing an indication of weather, season and time, and acting as a counterpoint to an otherwise harsh inner city environment. The ground floor lounge is set under a double height triangular lightwell to roof level, giving the sensation of height in a small space. The second bedroom upstairs is bathed in light from a light shaft, which projects to roof level. This light shaft provides a dramatic internal ambience and contributes to the overall sculptural form of the house. We are currently working with the Guardian newspaper to provide a digital newssheet as the new elevation for the neighbour-

ing shopfront.

AW

Your North London Community Centre seems to combine some of the ideas of the larger and smaller scale projects. How did this project start?

AYB

Our client wanted a commercial component and also a Muslim based community centre to form a major London landmark.

So we looked at five different schemes from something quite simple which just tried to resolve the commercial component, to something more complex. We started with a more volumetric design - essentially this is a nursing home, a children's play centre for toddlers, a small prayer area, a library and all kinds of other things – about 7,000 square metres in total. This project is quite tough, and builds up a high volume, with south facing terraces. We looked at the idea of an inhabited roof with these dropped courtyards which are taken from some examples in India, but a development of this thinking has been to adopt a softer geometry.

The scheme sets out to explore the richness and cultural variety with defines Islamic Architecture. The project is conceived as a soft undulating landscape reminiscent of the landscapes in the Muslim world, using courtyards, light, pattern, geometry and water as key design elements. The scheme will avoid the use of derivative symbols which have contributed much to the demise of Islamic architecture and instead we will provide contemporary Islamic architecture relevant to the British context. The aim will be to create open fluid spaces where activities are blurred and where one activity and use merges into another. The scheme will overlay activities in the building - for example to create areas where young children can sit in a courtyard alongside the elderly from the nursing home.

One of core aims of the project will be to invite and encourage dialogue between Muslims and the wider Non Muslim community. The NLC scheme is an inclusive project which will create dialogue through the use of spaces open to the public such restaurants, exhibition spaces, courtyard and terraces. NLC will be open to people of all ethnic and religious backgrounds.

Facades of Peabody Housing, Silvertown. An interview
with Niall McLaughlin of Niall McLaughlin Architects

NM -   Niall McLaughlin
JD -   Jeg Dudley

JD

Let's begin by talking about the low cost housing you've completed in Silvertown and the client for that project - the Peabody Housing Association. Did you find this organization imposed many constraints on you during the design process?

NM

Given the building type it was quite the opposite. The Peabody Trust set up what I thought was a very good competition in 2001, called 'Fresh Ideas for Low Cost Housing', and they asked practices with around seven or fewer people in them to apply. They asked questions about gender balance and ethnic balance and so on - so they were looking for small virtuous practices that were well run in a way. On the basis of that they made a shortlist of ten - what I'd call the usual suspects of my generation - and they sent out a very nice brief, which was 'here is the competition for a site - if you win the site you get to build it, but if you don't, don't worry about it because it's a calling card and I'm sure we'll come back to you again in due course'. So it was a very enlightened way of going about it.

It was a design and build project, but it involved partnering from the first stage, and they were really good builders - we're still friends with them now, years later. The Peabody Trust also had a relaxed approach - given that they are an organization and they have a very large amount of absolute standards which are published in documents and so on, after that they would lean back and say, 'well you're the experts - how would you solve this problem?'. And there were some issues in this project - for example the radiant light film that is part of the façade system is made by 3M, who don't make building components. So we had a major problem with the insurers, who reinsure for first time buyers. They asked who was going to supply a lifetime guarantee on it, and 3M said they certainly wouldn't. I think under that pressure a lot of other clients would have just said, 'go sort this out - find something else, or paint the stripes on or something'. But the Peabody Trust sort of said, 'you're grown-up boys, go and sort it out and then tell us what the solution is'. There was a kind of optimism and openness from them about being clients, which I think is very unusual.

JD

And to solve that problem you contacted the glass specialists Dewhurst MacFarlane, and ask them to draw up a performance specification which would ensure the material could be used?

View from street

View from street

NM

In a situation like that where a project is coming to site on a fixed programme, and you come across a potentially show-stopping problem, you want to approach it from as many fronts as possible. So on one hand we got Dewhurst MacFarlane to do some analysis on it and they boiled it down to only one thing that could go wrong: possible UV embrittlement of the glue that holds the radiant film in place. We then put UV film onto the glass and had Dewhurst MacFarlane re-examine it by doing accelerated UV testing on the new panels - but even at that speed the testing wasn't going to be complete until the project was well on site. So the other thing we did was we simply changed the detailing a little bit so that the performance of the radiant light film isn't implicated in the performance of the building from an insurer's point of view.

JD

The radiant light film is an interesting material - it's more often used for glossy wrapping or cosmetics packaging. How did it end up in the final design?

NM

Well we looked at the history of the area and found the site was in a sense a kind of 'lost site' - in about 1850 the whole place was a swamp with almost nothing there. The first time we get word of Silvertown is

View from street

that a man called Silver set up a rubber factory there in 1851 - we found this fascinating because that's the year of the great exhibition, the era of Victorian consumer durables and the idea of cheap raw materials being imported from the Empire, and then on the beach in Silvertown they built factories to convert those raw materials into cheap local ones.

JD

You've made references in the past to this long and varied list - "sugar, coloured dyes, jam, golden syrup, gutta percha, soda, TNT, soap and matches"...

NM

It's amazing, isn't it? So there's that idea of manufacturing cheap colour, cheap light and cheap sweetness that we found really interesting. The idea that suddenly luxury became cheap because of chemical manufacture.

And then the other thing we were interested in is that timber frame construction, which at the time was the way that almost all housing associations were going for low cost construction, is a funny thing. It's an industrialized building process in a sense - you put up these very quick and simple frames that make a box, then the box is insulated and it gets Tyvek on the out-

Applying and cutting dichroic film to the louvres for the glazed units

side and plasterboard on the inside. So in a sense it represents the performance of the building, and then depending on your taste you wrap it in something - conventionally most housing associations wrap it in brick or cedar cladding or something like that. But all they are trying to do is return what is an industrial product back into a quasi-natural state, or to make it look as though it was built in some other way. We wanted to say in a sort of gently ironic way that 'this is an industrial object which is being wrapped'.

At the time this rather beautiful thing came into the office - one of those TNT or ParcelForce packages - and it was a box, beautifully wrapped in brown paper, with various instructions added to it in coloured tape. It had 'Fragile - this way up' and 'Urgent: Overnight' and others around it, all in beautiful coloured paper, and then the whole thing was wrapped in bubblewrap. We thought, 'God, isn't that gorgeous' and we actually brought it to the interview and said 'this is what industrial wrapping is like'.

In the initial phase our cladding system was a balloon frame box, and we wanted to see through to the Tyvek because it's quite an interesting layer - so we were going to have twin-wall polycarbonate in front of it. Then we were going to simply wrap it with ribbons of different things. But a number of different problems came

Installing the glazed unit

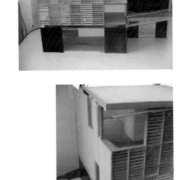

Working models

up with that - one of them was the ribbons felt a bit weak - they were a bit too literally like what we had been talking about. The other was that I had concerns myself that if you have a polycarbonate façade you have to ventilate up the back of it, as there's a danger of mould growth on the back of the polycarbonate where it's inaccessible. And you could see through to it, so it would look a mess.

We were kind of worrying about that, and then Martin Richman, who is an artist and an old friend of the office, and who hadn't been involved in the competition at all - came in to the office for something else. I just borrowed him and said, 'this is what we're doing, any suggestions?' He had this stuff called radiant light film in his bag at the time, there were some people in the office who just had the horrors when they saw it, because it just looked so cheap and tacky - like disco film. It's the kind of stuff you'd buy in a cheap shop for wrapping presents. So there was a concern that it would be far too tacky - but I felt that if it was properly structured you could do quite interesting things with it.

JD

You've been quite careful in your detailing - the black edges of the horizontal and vertical frame contrast with it, and the panels sit above a ground floor plinth of much darker brickwork.

Yes - that was quite a strong part of what we're doing. The particular part of Evelyn Road that was there was used for warehousing, and we liked the idea that these are like big packing crates, and at one stage we were looking at tea chests. We liked the idea of these big cubic plywood packing crates that are sitting on top of a podium that goes along and comes up and becomes a stairwell, so you have an implied four cubes sitting on this podium. And the reason we took the corners out of it is because of the views: one set of views down towards the Dome and Canary Wharf, and another towards London City Airport, which, if you are going to live there, are the things to look at. So that's why we made these corner windows.

In a way that's how we dealt with the idea of a robust podium. But in fact I was a bit concerned with the colour of the brick, and it was Martin who pushed me quite strongly in that direction, saying that the brick must be very flat and very dark because the thing that you want to sing out is the gorgeous object on top.

JD

It's interesting that you mention the flatness of the brick podium, because in contrast there is a depth to the film that seems to go beyond its physical shape. The radiant film is set in 'stepped' bands so that sometimes the light fades and these front and back layers of film merge into a flat plane, while at other times the sun picks at it in a certain way and it becomes very three dimensional and shimmers and moves.

When I saw them myself - on a typically dreary English winter's day - the buildings were literally 'radiant'. I definitely saw the analogies you've made in the past with peacocks feathers, or oil on water, and so on. You talk about 'recreating a chemical flare' with the façade.

NM

Well we had a great time making big plywood mock-ups in the office that represented one of the panels, putting different layers inside and working with all kinds of glass, and so on. Then we'd stick them up on a wall outside - there's a great photograph of us all lying on the ground out there, you can't see what we're looking at, but there's a colour haze over us from the reflected light!

There was also a lot of testing - we had 1:10 scale models of the façade and 1:1 scale bits made and there was a lot of tweaking it as we were making it. That maybe isn't something that a façade systems architect gets the chance to do as often. We felt more like we'd built this one ourselves rather than bought it from a catalogue.

At one stage I wanted to use Georgian wired glass in the panels. I quite like it, it's always used in lavatories and municipal buildings and has very negative connotations, but actually it's gorgeous. Unfortunately you can't put wired glass in a double glazed system, so we chose Georgian cast glass, which gives you a slightly pixelated affect. Maybe what you described has to do with that - the shifts from being a surface to having quite a strong depth. As it doesn't have a pure float glass surface, you get that slightly dimpled, very slightly diffuse feel from it. I liked it because if you look at it from one angle it becomes the dominant surface, but if you tilt it very slightly you see right through. You can see that as you come around the building - the colours die right off and it becomes like a grey screen with very subtle colours across it.

Rendering of project for St James's Church, Peckham

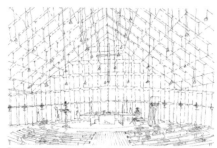
Sketch by Niall McLaughlin: St James's Church, Peckham

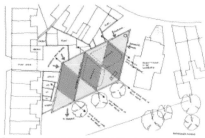
Sketch site plan showing glazed (blue) and solid (grey) roof areas

We were also quite interested in the checkerboard pattern that Lutyens did on the Peabody Housing in 1930, which AHMM did a homage to. We thought we would pick up on that and do our own version, but in our case the checkerboard works. There are two different kinds of panels using the blue and orange radiant light film - on the first panel they begin orange-blue-orange- and so on, and on the other panel the order is reversed. We didn't quite know how it would work, but we thought there would be potentially sixteen or eighteen different conditions of reflected light caused by the two different kinds of film and the reflective aluminium frames.

Then there were two other components - one is that on certain days you get this coloured carpet on the road. In the right conditions of light the tarmac road suddenly has this coloured carpet across it. And the other element was the silver birch trees in front - for us it was quite important that if you're in your flat you can look out and see the silver birches full of light. So the façade, the podium, the road and the silver birches allowed us to see the project as something that exists in all the elements.

The film really reacts to whatever it is reflecting direct-

ly opposite. Maybe one of the disadvantages of that site is that it's quite open ground opposite - if you had a complex row of mixed London houses opposite the thing would be going bananas, because it does very strange things to reflections.

JD

This project seems to be quite distinct from your past work. Many of your buildings are preoccupied with light, but they use their form and geometry to produce the desired effect. For example, on the small shack for a photographer you built a series of flexing, perforated canopies that resembled insects wings for the roof - these gently moved to produce varied lighting effects. On this project, however, the effect is achieved through just a surface treatment.

It is certainly true that light is used here in a way that is entirely different to the way it is used in other projects. The shack is a really good example, you go in there and it's some kind of strange light-box, it works well because it's a kind of pavilion or folly - you go down to visit the light. But if you are doing houses for people the light has to become more typical and more about the times of the day: I like the idea of walking in and finding an openness that doesn't feel like you've been

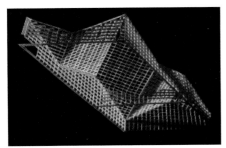
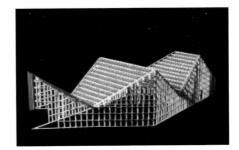

Working models: St James's Church, Peckham

pre-empted in any way. In a sense I wanted the layouts to be typical rather than bespoke and particularized in any way. I think the specifics of light tend to do that, they require that degree of complexity in their generation.

There is always a bit of me that wonders about the complete matter-of-factness of the arrangement of the interiors, and then the rather extra-ordinary facades - for me I'm never sure whether that's an entirely easy arrangement. As a south facing façade on a house it's okay for this thing to reflect light away, and to make a song and dance about it. But I feel as though there isn't a complete integration between the spatial intensity of the interior and this façade. At the time I was reading Semper for the first time and I was quite interested, as I guess many people are these days, in what Bötticher called Kernform and Kunstform. The core form, which is the construction and the thing it's actually built out of, is in this case the balloon frame. And then there's the Kunst form, which is in a sense a metaphor: there is some sort of tropism involved, it's a figure, a representation of something concealed. What that theory tends to do is generate a separation between the art form and the core form - I think this building does that too.

I wonder whether the revised interest in Semper that you get with all of these current facades that come from a sort of Swiss-German tradition - people like Herzog & de Meuron - is in one way a response to having to drive up the insulation value of buildings. Because what you end up with is a core building, which just does what it does, which is then wrapped in a duvet of insulation and outside that you have to put something which is so physically and mechanically distant from the core form, that in a sense it can be like a veil. It seems to me that this is something that has comes back because of the demands for high insulation and low energy use.

Facades of Recent Projects. An interview with Simon
Beames and Simon Dickens of youmeheshe

SD   Simon Dickens
SB-   Simon Beames
AW -   Andrew Watts

AW

How did you become involved with the Cutty Sark
project?

SB

I have worked on the Cutty Sark Restoration Project
since 2004. The way the project came into the office
was quite interesting. Nick Grimshaw was on BBC Ra-
dio's Desert Island Discs speaking to Sue Lawley and
said '..my passion is boats and if I hadn't have been
an architect I would have been a boat builder'. The
next day he had a letter from the Cutty Sark saying
they had a boat that needs fixing, adding 'why don't
you come and have a look'. So that was the start of
the project, and I worked on the project for a year or
so, after which time we managed to obtain a grant
from the Heritage Lottery Fund. Simon Dickens and I
decided to set up our office at this time, Youmeheshe,
and after a month we got a call from the Cutty Sark
saying that they would like us to continue working on
the project. Grimshaws found the mechanics to allow
us to be part of the team working on the project from
September 2005, as part of the extended Grimshaw
family.

The essential move was to raise the ship by about

three metres from its current position, glazing the
gap between the edge of the existing dry berth and
the ship, which is a form that has a complex geometry.
Buro Happold revisited a piece of structural analysis
undertaken by Greenwich University. Professor Chris
Bailey, a mathematician at the university, undertook
a finite element analysis of the ship to determine the
possibilities of the existing ship structure. This study is
constantly updated as we will not know enough about
the existing structure until we start to mobilise the final scheme. In effect, Cutty Sark's capabilities have
been calculated in advance prior to any physical work
being done to the ship. The ship itself was designed
with extraordinary skill. The Cutty Sark was built as
a sort of Ford Transit Van of the oceans; it was sup-
posed to do several trips back and forth to China, re-
turning as quickly as possible, with a five year life span.
However, it was a lavish Transit Van, costing £17,000
to build at the time. The form was refined by designer,
Hercules Linton, a composite structure, incredibly
light and strong, sailing as fast as possible. It could hit
big waves at speed – it was a tough vessel. The cargo
was worth £100,000 on its first journey, so its first
trip paid for the cost of construction five times over,
like the equivalent of a successful dot com business
today. At the time you wanted to build as many Cutty

Spatial distribution within entrance area

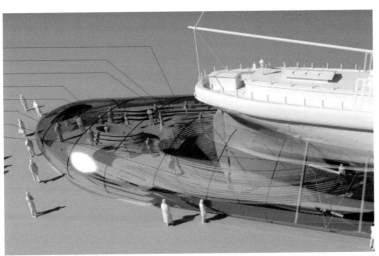

Aerial view of entrance

Sarks as possible!

AW

Was the form of the Visitor's Centre inspired by the form of the Cutty Sark?

SD

In the dry berth we are creating new visitor accommodation from an engineered timber form and this is formed in the shape of the vortices formed at the back of the ship when it was going at full speed – bearing in mind that speed was critical to the success of ships like the Cutty Sark. It is formed as a series of stacked timber sections. The ship itself sits within a dry berth constructed in the 1950s and was constructed to house the ship. Key features include the concrete dry berth, five metres deep. The ship currently sits on its keel, and is propped on its sides, causing the hull to sag and become disfigured. We are creating a new structure at ground level that will connect with the ship at 'tween deck levels, which is the strongest part of the ship. The compression struts continue across the ship beneath the between deck and tie back through to beyond the dry berth with tension piles, running the length of the ship and that is what holds the ship up. In order to create less pressure on the hull, we think that the hull could support itself, with a series of elements internally which return to the keel. The ship is holding itself, not the weight of the ship above it. So the supporting structure is completely distinct from the vessel, in this way you can read an articulated armature against the fantastic wrought iron frame of the existing ribs. As I said, the new structure is an accommodation block. Its form freezes the vortices of the water flow behind the ship, as a physical interpretation of the speed of the ship and is built in this way since we are representing the

status of engineering timber construction now, using computers in order to develop a relationship between CAD and CAM in order to give visitors a realisation that the ship was constructed using the most modern technique of the day and that this is what we can do as architects and engineers today.

AW

How was CAD and CAM used to develop the design?

SB

We used CAD software to develop this structure as a ruled line surface of 'contours'. This structure was conceived as a series of contours which stack. It was difficult to achieve and the first solution did not provide a smooth surface. So what we have now is a hierarchy, with a frame that supports a thick cladding. We have developed this surface, so that although the geometry follows the flow analysis of the water around the ship, we will achieve this with a series of inclined columns which sit within the timber structure itself. So although the form is unorthodox it is conventionally built. The tricky thing is to ensure each layer sits snugly onto the one below and achieve the simplicity required for construction. The drawings cut a solid model into sections. A 5-axis cutting machine can cut each piece to provide a smooth surface along each of the contours. The final part of the story is that the stairs set out the depth of each one of the contours. The new steps are set over the existing steps with the void between the two providing a service void between them. This area provides a snug working service hub to the Visitor Centre. Building a boat would have been easier! Builders don't always think about complex 3D forms in terms of the available machinery so there is a lot of testing to be done in order to encourage manufacturers to understand that their machines are

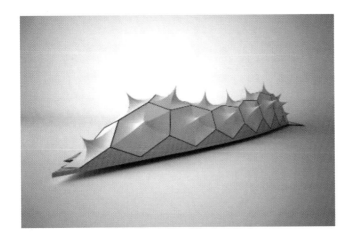

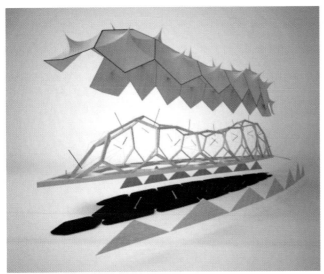

Concept studies for temporary museum

capable of constructing forms like this. I think it will be difficult to read the complexity of the design when the structure is installed.. As architects we are spending much time resolving issues geometrically and ensuring that it works before it goes to fabricators. We work hard to ensure that we provide a design that does not narrow the market, so that a well meaning timber craftsman can put it together. The craftsman may have to buy the equipment to read ouru files, but he doesn't necessarily have to design with the equipment or software to construct our forms, and that will be the same on many of other projects in the future. You need well meaning people – they don't have to be experts in the field for us to know that they can deliver what we are trying to achieve. As architects we aim to tease out their full potential. A 3D model passed back and forth between contractor and architect, which was unheard of until a few years ago. The model has been modified to create an efficient and economic 3D structure. We have to work in a way that does not double up on contractor design(clients won't pay twice for design) but interacts with contractors and provides the information they need to develop the scheme to completion.

AW

I understand that a parametric geometry was used to develop the form of the Temporary Visitor Centre.

SB

The use of MicroStation Generative Components (GC) to develop the parametric design came from our working at Grimshaws as well as teaching at the Architectural Association School here in London. As a small office we felt it was too ambitious for us to prototype on that scale but we could afford to be less precious about certain components and could invest

in GC. It was very successful. We worked closely with the engineers Buro Happold on the surface form finding of the external envelope. The fabric structure was developed in conjunction with the fabricators Base Structures, mainly with Windward Dexter, who undertook the structural analysis of the fabric. GC, as parametric software, worked well because the site is very specific geometrically and we could set simple geometric parameters, in section and in plan, and could create a form that found the maximum volume for the site we were given. The constraints for the parametric model were the Cutty Sark itself, the route of the London Marathon around the ship, and the adjacent pub. The London Marathon recently ran passed the building for the first time, so that obviously worked!

The next part of the Generative Components work was to develop a particular component for the building – a cone – which is differentiated by its position on the surface and its ability to use a stack effect as a trickle vent through the top of the spike and the area of patch it is sitting on. So the component was a sort of witches hat shape which was set across the surface. The array gave the basic position of the form of the fabric. Originally it was conceived as something which fits very closely to the armature or the structure which is a particular structure, but as we evolved the scheme with Base, who used their own form finding software for the fabric, we found that component size as provided by GC was bigger than that which the contractor considered was actually required. The contractor helped us to evolve the timber strut into something more beautiful. MicroStation Generative Components allowed us to develop and reconfigure the variables, of which there at least 10 versions created over a short period of time. Tender for the project took place in December 2006, with the Temporary Visitor Centre being completed by April, so for a building of such

Interior view of prefabicated timber unit

complexity, to get contractors up to speed, the digital tools used for the scheme were very successful. The contractors understood what we were wanting achieve. We were also quite demanding of the timber fabricators. We had sought a timber node, like a traditional Japanese construction, in a non hierarchical assembly of components, with struts held in place by friction. Due to the complexity, a mild steel ball-type connector was used instead and an hierarchical strategy developed. But even then, Gordon Cowley, of Cowley Timberwork, reduced the sizes of timber struts,

which made them visually much more elegant. This was a fantastic contribution to the project.

AW

The proposed glass enclosure to the Cutty Sark is visually stunning. Is very expensive?

SB

The glass being used on the Cutty Sark has been provided by Sunglas through Seele. The overall form is a double curvature, and we have attempted to form this using 3D CAD software in order to reduce the amount of indivual panel curvature while providing as much visual smoothness as possible. We have developed with them a system of clamping glass so that we can achieve mechanical curvature which is 75% of the enclosure, enough to curve 4000mm long panels by 150mm over their length, which is sufficient to follow the ship's lines. This amount is on a pro rata basis, so we can twist the glass where needed by 75mm over 2000mm. It would cost as much as a regular flat system by bonding the glass without the expense of pre-heating. We are using a ratio of 25% curving with heat in the factory and 75% bending of the panels on site. The glass is fixed in a pressure plate arrangement. Continuous pressure is applied along two parallel sides because of the bending involved.

AW

Did you consider other concepts for enclosing the ship structure?

SB

Originally we designed the structure to enclose the Cutty Sark which was more exciting, real innovation; an air beam structure which covered the entire ship, constructed of 1.5m diameter tubular struts to enclose the entire ship. That was the original scheme to provide a temporary visitors centre, any work we did for fabric pavilion was self motivated, its our own project.

SD

The original design had screw piles, which was not practical. This was quickly changed to a concrete slab with services set within the depth. There was no time to complete the design of the services so conduits were put down quickly. A fast and flexible process was required. We were disappointed to have to use PVC

as a membrane, because of its poor sustainability credentials. We prefer to use low energy materials.

AW

You are obviously making a landmark project here. Has this holistic approach fed into other projects?

SB

We used these principles to generate another project of ours, a prefabricated house. The traditional role of the architect delivering a service is changing. You now have to be fleet on your feet and be able to use your skills in other ways. So we have developed a design for a modular house and we are looking at being partners in development and placing this on various sites. From an external envelope point of view, this meets 'passivehaus' standards which requires no energy to heat it, so the performance of the envelope is the important feature of this building in order to ensure that heat is kept in the building, but the fascinating thing is that it has far more glass in the walls than current 'green' guidelines would suggest. We are putting a version of this design in a scheme of 26 houses in Stavanger, Norway. Here the dwellings have a view of the fjord below while being allocated an optimum orientation of solar collecting windows in relation to the sun and also optimise the view towards the fjord, in this way the house components can be altered to optimise their efficiency. Each of the 26 houses has a slightly different configuration with relationship to the site.

SD

This is where the use of our parametric CAD software, namely MicroStation Generative Components, again becomes relevant to our work. The houses are made as flat panels which come together at different angles, and are CNC cut. An area of Austria, where

The design of prefabicated timber units

they specialise in timber construction, has around 80 fabrication plants of which half are capable of doing this sort of construction from digital information and even these don't look like digital fabrication type factories. We are trying to get that technology here in the UK and convince companies to work here, or convince people here that the technology exists. In fact our research and technology comes through doing our work in Stavanger, where they have just realised that that their timber construction is from a 200 year old recipe. In Stavanger they have recently looked over their shoulder and seen that other countries are delivering things in a 21st Century way, and that they need to catch up. We have managed to collaborate with a Norwegian company and they are helping a developer set up a factory in Norway to help deliver solid timber panels in the country. We are trying to break into the United States with this project, and have received a

high level of interest to date.

AW

How does the low energy design create a stuffy internal environment?

SB

This is a passive house – low energy. We are looking at creating a healthier environment both inside the buildings and outside. This is the way buildings will have to go, using technology to achieve this.

SD

The walls of our prefabricated house are of solid timber panels with 300mm thermal insulation around them. We are creating a 'vacuum flask', using heat from the earth to keep the building warm. A heat exchanger and ground source heat pump are used to supply heat energy. We have to get that knowledge over here in the UK.

SB

When we were introduced to this technology we became evangelised about it and realised that it is almost a crime that every architect,, every engineer, is not delivering buildings that are heated in this way. There is no excuse for schools, being constructed all over the country today, not being heated by passive means. The earth is at a constant 10 degrees Celsius in this country. Why are we not mobilising heat energy and directing it through a heat exchanger to deliver the right environment – which is super fresh? The first time we stood in a passive house it was virtually a religious experience. Such an environment is like being outside in terms of the freshness of the air, perhaps as all the air coming into the building is filtered and constantly replaced. We are used to being in a shut, double glazed environment with radiators pumping out heat, where the humidity is terrible, the quality of the air is terrible, especially with the use of trickle vents. A passive house is constantly flushed, the air is never stagnated as it moves through the house. The heat is exchanged from the air going out to the air coming in. It feels exactly the right temperature but the air is fresher. An ambition for our work is that we want to cover the world in these houses so that everyone can enjoy the experience! We have ensured that the Cutty Sark Visitor Centre has ground source heat pumps. We are part of a group that will build a set of houses off the Old Kent Road. We want this to be a proof to developers who will be able to see all this. We have to build these houses or move to Austria!

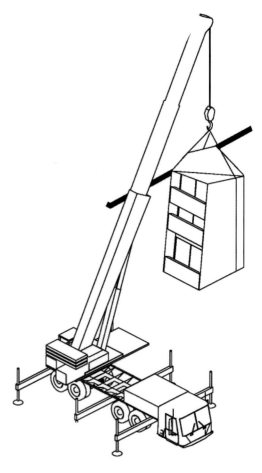

View of prefabicated timber units

4_ projects

Client: Lyford Investments Ltd
Contractor: Phase 1: Unimead Ltd (ground works and frame)
Phase 2: Kaymac Construction (envelope and fit-out)
Structural Engineer: Price & Myers
Services Consultant : Peter Deer & Associates

alison brooks
architects
project:
houses
lyford road, london sw18
nearest tube:
clapham south

The Herringbone Houses are two 400sqm houses and integrated landscape located in a wooded back land site overlooking the South London Bowls Club for private developer Lyford Investments.

Each open-plan house is composed of two continuous planes of herringbone timber and graphite render surfaces that form walls, floors, external decking and fences. These planes interlock and fold inward at the centre of the house to create a double height entrance hall open to the sky. This approach to the wrapping of spaces generates an apparent lightness to the houses which are conceived as an assembly of planar elements as opposed to "punched" masonry. The atrium holds a suspended timber staircase and galleries which lead to the first and second floor bedrooms. Each house has a two car carport that has been integrated into the design of the house, fence and landscape with pebbled roofs on expanded metal trays supported by stainless steel 'picture frames'.

The 3 storey, 5 bedroom, houses have full basements with storage, guest accommodation and a games room. The ground floor is conceived as an open plan living, family and kitchen wrapped around a central double height hall open to the sky with a 3x2m roof

View of balcony

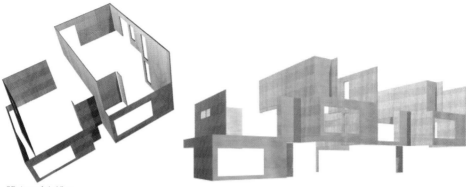

3D views of cladding

View of houses

Rendered view of houses

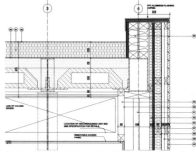

Section detail at roof parapet and front window (typical)

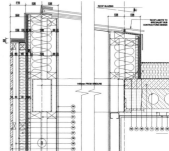

Typical section detail at roof light 1, 2nd floor

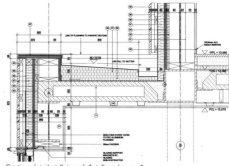

Section detail at flat roof, 1st floor house 1

light. The hall is a double height atrium at the centre of the house with a sculptural oak staircase hanging in the middle of the space. The first floor bedrooms are accessed from a gallery space and library with a balcony offering views down into the living space.

The three principle bedrooms are on the west facing façade with large windows that maximise passive solar gain and offer fantastic views out over the bowling green. All of the bedrooms have windows on both sides to allow natural ventilation of the spaces and maximise the light and views. The living rooms are recessed behind deep overhangs that provide shade, direct views to the south-east and shelter the ground floor entrance areas. Adjacent to these are the three storey volumes oriented north south, containing bedrooms and family rooms. These elements also have recessed glazing at the 2nd floor level to reduce solar gain, increase a sense of privacy for the occupants and create space for greenery at the buildings upper levels.

The ground floor living spaces have been designed in order to create a free flowing space from inside to outside with level thresholds opening out to generous terraces.

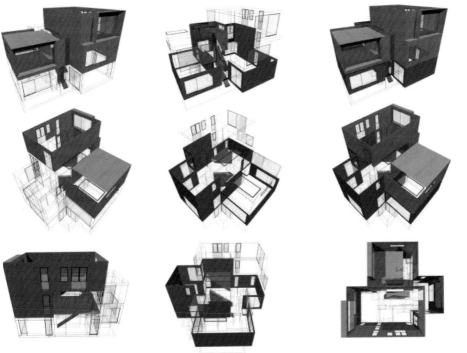

Volumetric views of houses

The house is constructed from a steel frame with timber infill that has been wrapped in plywood sheathing. This acts as a substrate for the insulation and cladding. The herringbone cladding was initially developed and set out using 3d modelling software to establish the dimension of each board and to test the final visual effect. After trials with different lengths of board and widths it was decided to us a thin board profile (50mm) and that the boards should be 800mm long,

a dimension that worked functionally for the construction and fitted into the structural levels of the house.

The cladding is essentially a traditional open weatherboard construction, the house being initially wrapped in Tyvek breather paper over the rigid insulation. Battens were set out at 800mm horizontal centres and the IPE cladding was all pre-cut to

Timber cladding being installed

Mock-ups of cladding

800mm lengths with pre-drilled holes to speed up the installation and accuracy of the construction process. At the architect's request the contractor constructed a 1:1 mock-up to test the construction of the façade and each stage of the installation was signed off by the architect before proceeding. This enabled the architect to maintain a tight control over the building finish. Following the installation of the boards each board was pelleted and sanded before sign off.

Across the façade all materials Timber, Render and Glass are in the same plane. This was done to further enhance the abstract planar quality of the façade. The windows sit on steel angles and are strapped back to the window heads and jams, meaning that they can be positioned flush with the timber, like holes cut out of in a thin surface.

Given the automation of the process and simplicity of the traditional construction method this delicate and refined façade took no longer and cost no more than a standard horizontal weatherboarding system. Yet the result is a distinctive façade with an optical 'accordion' effect and with the refinement of a piece of renaissance marquetry.

Volumetric views of houses

Views of herringbone texture of facades

allford hall
monaghan morris
project:
southwark child
development centre
peckham way, london se18
nearest rail:
queens road (peckham)

Client: Building Better Health
Contractor: Willmott Dixon
Structural Engineer: Price & Myers
Services Consultant : WhitbyBird

The Southwark Child Development Centre is a new children's Primary Care centre situated on Peckham Road in South London. The building brings together under one roof the services currently provided in three different locations, including purpose built facilities for children with special needs. It aims to provide a stimulating and appropriate environment for child health services drawing on examples of best practice elsewhere.

The variety of services provided requires a range of different room types, each of a prescribed and differing size and with complex relationships that produce a naturally irregular internal plan. However, the highly constrained site sits amongst dark brick mansion blocks of uniform and monolithic scale. Responding to this context, the building thus initially takes the form of a dark glazed brick block, a simple rectangle in plan and stepped rectangle in elevation, rising from three storeys to six and cantilevering as it meets St Giles' Road. Resolving the interplay between the complex and colourful internal arrangement and the formal urban envelope is the main driver for the façade design.

In order to achieve this, a limited palette of devices is deployed in a range of ways.

Brise-soleil panels

Brickwork prior to completion

View of model

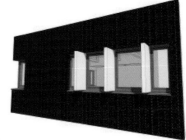

Volumetric views of facades

Firstly, the dark brick block is shown to be only a thin skin. Long horizontal window cuts reveal a staccato pattern of mullions which corresponds to the irregular room layout. Aluminium side-hung casement windows are set back behind the skin and allow the reveals to act by name, exposing the bricks' overall thinness.

Voids cut out behind the skin then break down the interior volume while allowing the exterior massing to remain intact. The upper level voids create private outdoor terraces which provide natural daylight and ventilation to rooms deep within the building. Nevertheless, they are opened to public view through unglazed openings in the facade, lined in brightly coloured render which is also expressed as a layer with its own thickness.

Voids cut between the three public lower levels are similarly lined in colour. These, however, are internal spaces which enable views between the floors to help visitors orientate themselves. As public elements their linings are brought out through the brick façade to address the street and welcome visitors, forming external sunshades, sheltered play areas, and the main building entrance.

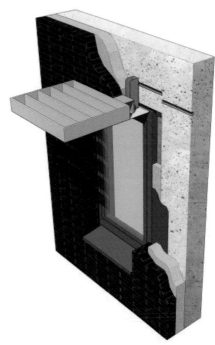

Volumetric view around window opening

View of model

Rendered view from street

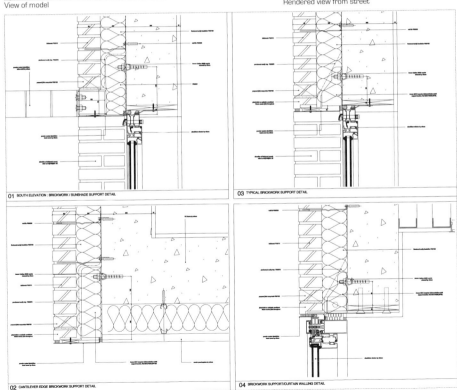

01 SOUTH ELEVATION : BRICKWORK / SUNSHADE SUPPORT DETAIL

03 TYPICAL BRICKWORK SUPPORT DETAIL

02 CANTILEVER EDGE BRICKWORK SUPPORT DETAIL

04 BRICKWORK SUPPORT/CURTAIN WALLING DETAIL

Typical details through facade

Long elevation

This principle of pulling brightly coloured elements through the façade is then continued on the upper windows. Here bright sky-blue brise-soleil spring from within the window cuts. These are expressed as simple orthogonal elements: horizontal and louvred to the south, vertical and solid to the east and west. They orient their visible surfaces to catch and reflect direct sunlight, preventing overheating and animating the facade. To the north, where no brise-soleil are required, the window frames themselves are bright blue, again expressing the building's colourful inner life.

Technically the construction looks deceptively traditional, following the basic principle of a cavity wall with full-fill insulation. However, the inner leaf is a solid and continuous reinforced concrete wall. This acts as a massive shear structure to support the building cantilever, provides integral lintels for long horizontal strip windows, and supports a variety of stainless steel bracketry to carry the thin skin brickwork, which otherwise could not take its own weight. Plastered internally, the concrete also provides thermal mass, slowing the building's heating and cooling cycle and helping the rooms within to be warm in winter, cool in summer. As with the activities within, although this appears to be a simple building, much is going on behind the scenes.

The façade thus embodies the philosophy of building: local but distinctive, strong but playful; a colourful but urbane solution to a rich and often conflicting set of programme and performance requirements.

Views of construction on site

ash sakula
architects
project:
peabody trust housing
silvertown, london e16
nearest tube:
west silvertown dlr

Client: Peabody Trust
D & B Contractor: Sandwood Construction
Structural Engineer: Whitbybird
Services Engineer: Atelier Ten

This housing project of four apartment units is a prototype development that grew out of a winning entry in a Peabody Trust competition for 'fresh ideas' for affordable new housing on three infill sites in east London, with a competition brief:

"to explore new ideas that really address how best to deliver value to people who are starting on the bottom rung of home ownership. . . . wonderful places to live, reflecting the allusions perhaps of a more upmarket end of home ownership, with a design-led sense of spaciousness, light and style."

The architects consider the scheme to be innovative because it rethinks what a minimum-sized dwelling should be and how the dwellings should be linked: proposing radical new ideas for its layout, how space should be prioritised, what it should look like and how it should be constructed. They consider the solution to be one that represents a radical reappraisal of the domestic space priorities of the traditional small flat with an unconventional but extremely workable spatial arrangement.

Consequently, the entrance doubles as a very large balcony. A place large enough for six people to gather round a table. The hall is a 'sorting zone'. It is spacious, complex, not serving only as a corridor. The Kitchen is the main social space of the flat and is generous.

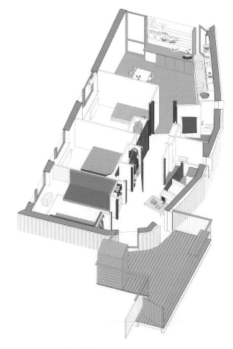

Isometric view of typical apartment

View of facade

View of facade

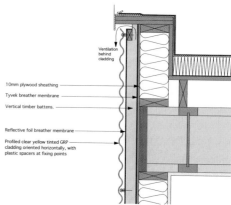

10mm plywood sheathing

Tyvek breather membrane

Vertical timber battens.

Reflective foil breather membrane

Profiled clear yellow tinted GRP
cladding oriented horizontally, with
plastic spacers at fixing points

Ventilation
behind
cladding

Consequently, the living room becomes a (with)Drawing room: cosier than the kitchen for TV, music and friends and it can also be used as home office or guest room. Bedrooms are as small as possible: clothes are stored in the sorting zone. The WC and bathroom are separated, both are large and naturally lit and ventilated. The staircase between the units becomes a communal space and vertical garden, storing bikes and bins under.

The plan of each unit is basically identical, with some re-orientation of windows and two alternative but adjacent front door positions. The curved tapering shape of the resultant pod with its ability to be configured in an almost infinite variety of ways around differing access arrangements make it ideally suited to small and irregular sites - here a small, acute angled triangle.

Internally, the small, compact, separate living room allowed the architects to create more than one social focus to the flat - a more intimate room than the larger kitchen space. The room works as a (with)drawing room for talking, drinking, arguing and watching TV. The other social space, the kitchen, can be seen right from the front hall through a wide door. When coming into the space, the far corner offers a sense of release just where a dead end might be expected, either through a real door in the ground floor flats or else with a full height window with plunging views out

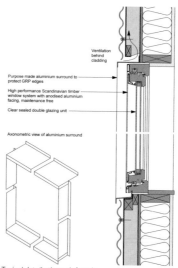

Ventilation
behind
cladding

Purpose made aluminium surround to
protect GRP edges

High performance Scandinavian timber
window system with anodised aluminium
facing, maintenance free

Clear sealed double glazing unit

Axonometric view of aluminium surround

Typical details through facade

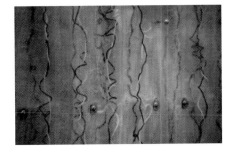

Views of cladding construction on site

View of entrance to housing units

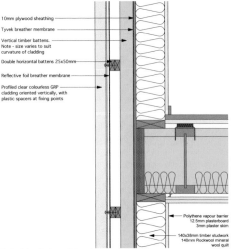

10mm plywood sheathing

Tyvek breather membrane

Vertical timber battens.
Note - size varies to suit
curvature of cladding

Double horizontal battens 25x50mm

Reflective foil breather membrane

Profiled clear colourless GRP
cladding oriented vertically, with
plastic spacers at fixing points

Polythene vapour barrier
12.5mm plasterboard
3mm plaster skim

140x38mm timber studwork
140mm Rockwool mineral
wool quilt

Typical details through facade

to the street from the upper floors. The kitchen is an adaptable space large enough to take a couple of extra elements like a comfortable chair and a playpen as well as a dining table and chairs.

The project also combined an integrated and innovative approach to materials, specification and construction, aimed at economy, speed, sustainability and comfort. The units were assembled on site using a maximum of prefabricated elements to achieve speed and quality in the construction and can be stacked from one up to seven storeys high. In this project the pods are in two 2-storey stacks, linked by a steel and timber staircase and deck structure that provides access and outside space to the upper flats and defines a communal space between all the flats.

In terms of construction and sustainability, the materials were chosen for their durability and lightness, and lower embodied energy. The transparent profiled GRP

sheets used over a silver reflective breather membrane are extremely durable. To the front the walls are clad in pale yellow tinted sheets oriented horizontally and the curved rear walls are clad in clear transparent sheet oriented vertically so accommodating the curve of this elevation. This lightweight rainscreen is installed over highly insulated timber cassette wall panels, these were manufactured off site and delivered ready for assembly. The composite timber joists used for floor and roof structures give additional rigidity, allowing for future flexibility.

High quality, high performance timber windows to the south and west gather useful solar energy and minimise heat loss and with the powder coated aluminium facings make external maintenance minimal. A steel/timber deck access structure with balustrades combining timber posts with chainlink fencing details allows the growth of vertically spreading planting.

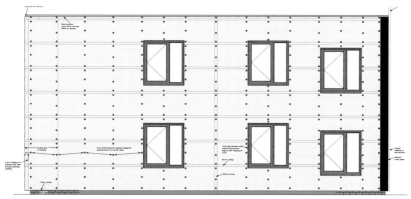

Drawing showing setting out of cladding

View of entrance to housing units

cottrell & vermeulen

Client: London Borough of Lewisham
Contractor: Buxton Building Contractors Ltd
Structural Engineer: Engineers HRW
Services Consultant : Downie Consulting Engineers

project:
bellingham fyp
gateway building
brookehowse rd, london se6
nearest rail: bellingham

The Bellingham Families and Young People's Gateway
building is located at the corner of Bellingham playing
field in south London.

The building accommodates facilities for Lewisham
Youth Service, Gateway facilities for the Bellingham
Recreation Project and a 0-15 month Sure Start
nursery.

The building is conceived as part of the landscape and
is designed to make a minimum impact on the open
space. This achieved by the use of a sedum roof and
translucent cladding materials.

The street side is clad in translucent GRP that reflects
and creates shadows formed by the park trees, creating a changing subtle street architecture.

The new Bellingham Families and Young People's
Gateway building is located at the corner of Bellingham playing field in south London, and provides new
accommodation for activities existing on the site as
well as bringing new activities and resources to the
area. The Sport England site, at Bellingham Fields in
South East London, was previously designated as metropolitan open land. For this reason location was key

Views of model

View of front entrance

Views of construction on site

View of external cladding

Main entrance elevation

projects_cottrell & vermeulen

in establishing an approach and obtaining consents. Strategically the new centre operates as a 'stepping stone', developing on the edge of the fields on the opposite side from the existing Bellingham Sports Centre. Conceived as an interconnected centre, the building offers an opportunity for users and resources to overlap and inter-relate. It is a new type of local building that encourages participation of all ages with local activities. The building accommodates facilities for Lewisham Youth Service, Gateway facilities for the Bellingham Recreation Project and a 0-15 months nursery for Bellingham Sure Start. The sport related element is intended to supplement existing provision, offering a less intimidating environment in which local residents aged between 8 and 19 years can discover a range of physical activities. The nursery provides a care for the very young and integrates with the local Sure Start facilities with the wider Community of Bellingham. At 57metres long and 12.5m deep, the linear form building contains a youth centre at its north end, a babies' nursery at the south end and a shared reception to the middle. The building geometry is cranked twice along its length reflecting the different uses internally, but additionally the change in profile along its spine reduces its overall scale.

On the playing field side the building is conceived as part of the landscape and is designed to make a minimum impact on the open space, achieved by the use of a sedum roof and translucent cladding materials. A high level fence, required to protect the building from the football fields adjacent, will eventually become softened with climbing planting. The street side is clad in translucent GRP that reflects and creates shadows formed by the park trees that form a changing subtle street architecture. At low level this is combined with an eternit profile sheet of the same profile. It was felt important to eliminate any fences to the entrance and for this reason the building itself forms a variable boundary to the street, unhostile, open but protected. Strict budget constraints forced a shortening of the building, whereby sports room activities were reorganised. In addition the amount of green roof was reduced - however in both cases the architect sought to maintain initial strategic aims in the final realisation. A rapid construction programme of 32 weeks was initially considered unrealistic. However good co-ordination with the contractor, especially regarding the setting out of the steel frame, allowed a relatively smooth construction period and the building was delivered on time and on budget.

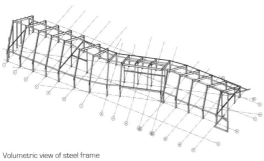

Volumetric view of steel frame

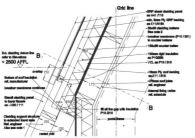

Typical External Wall Section 1 : 10
(A) Street facing, 65 pitch roof

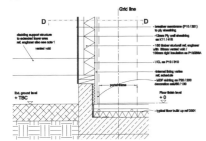

Typical external wall section

Views of construction on site

Views of Bellingham FYP Gateway Building

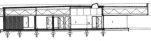

Section through the Lloyd Park Centre

Views of the Lloyd Park Centre and the design process with the local community

The Lloyd Park Centre

The Lloyd Park Centre is a striking new building situated near the William Morris Gallery in Walthamstow, London. It is home to the children's centre and nursery with the same name; an independent, parent-led organisation which inhabited the site in Portakabins for almost 20 years. The building is conceived as a 'pavilion in the park' - a rounded shape with outdoor access from most rooms and 'incisions' to create covered play areas. The building is decorated with a screen-printed pattern, developed in collaboration with the children and local artists and drawing on the wallpaper printing techniques of William Morris. Internally, materiality and simplicity drive the design, using exposed trussed rafters, oriented strand board and plenty of pin board for spontaneous decoration by staff and children. Sliding partitions between rooms encourages flexibility of use by the many different user groups, with acoustic ceiling panels and wall insulation to mitigate noise. The deep rafters create a high and a low ceiling height, high-level storage and generous space for service ducts and equipment.

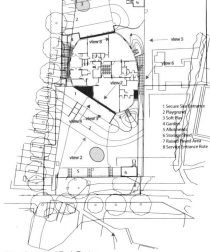

1 Secure Site Entrance
2 Playground
3 Soft Play
4 Garden
5 Allotments
6 Storage Shed
7 Raised Paved Area
8 Service Entrance Rote

Plan of the Lloyd Park Centre

Models of the Lloyd Park Centre

introduction
essays
interviews
4 _projects

dRMM

Client: Lambeth Education
Contractor: Ashe Construction (Southern) Ltd
Structural Engineer: Michael Hadi Associates
Services Engineer: Fulcrum Consulting

project:
clapham manor
primary school
belmont road, london sw4
not yet constructed

Clapham Manor Primary School, a successful primary school with reception and nursery, approached dRMM in 2003 with plans to become a two-form entry school to meet the increasing demands of the local community. The survival of the school depended on the addition of new classrooms and the remodelling of existing ones to cope with student levels.

The school is within a conservation area and the only available site that would not further encroach on the limited playground space for the pupils is adjacent to the listed Oddfellows Hall. These delicate site conditions required careful consideration, in addition to the need to rationalise the accommodation and provide accessible circulation.

The resultant proposal is for a four storey extension within the height of the existing three storey Victorian school. The proposed new extension is set back from the existing Victorian school and linked via a glazed connection. The extension will relieve pressure for space within the existing building, and allow remodelling of internal classrooms within the Victorian school such that teaching areas are within government guidelines.

Internal view of typical classroom

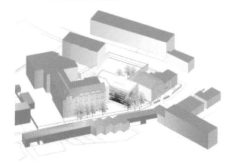

3D visual: site and proposed building

Planning model: view from playground

Planning model: view from Stonhouse Street / main entrance

West Elevation: planning proposal showing colour scheme

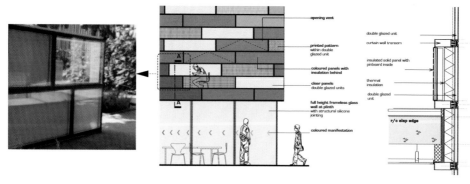

2. curtain wall facade sample scale 1:1

3. curtain wall facade elevation scale 1:50

3. curtain wall section detail A-A scale 1:10

Detail external elevation: Curtain wall

1. mock-up facade sample scale 1:1

1:1 sample mock-ups (W 1000mm, H 800mm, D 160mm)

The site to the north of the Victorian school was chosen for the new extension after one year of consultation and completion of a feasibility study investigating possible sites within the school boundary. This site was occupied by a redundant 1950's two storey caretaker's house, a 1970's three storey administration extension to the original Victorian school block, a canopy, a ramp and a hard landscaped surround. This built-upon site was favoured since the school already has very little outdoor play space (well below current government guidelines), and building elsewhere would have resulted in reduction of this already limited play area. Furthermore, a characteristic of the school's

success is that all its teaching spaces are under one roof. In keeping with this ethos, the new accommodation connects directly to the Victorian school, via the glazed link.

The appearance of the extension - height, massing and façade treatment - evolved through both technical and aesthetic considerations, and through a process of community consultation and close cooperation with Lambeth Planning and Conservation departments. The footprint and massing have been reduced at the request of the conservation officer to lessen the visual impact of the development. Floor levels have been restructured to result in a much more compact building,

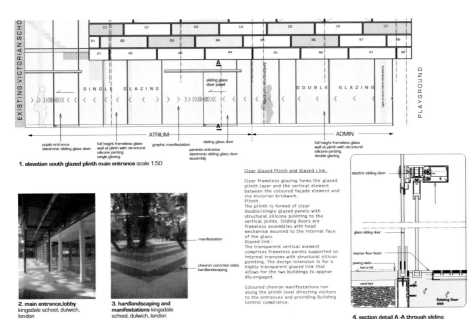

1. elevation south glazed plinth main entrance scale 1:50

pupils entrance
electronic sliding glass door

full height frameless glass
wall at plinth with structural
silicone jointing.
single glazing

graphic manifestation

sliding glass door

parents entrance
electronic sliding glass door
assembly

full height frameless glass
wall at plinth with structural
silicone jointing.
double glazing

2. main entrance, lobby
kingsdale school, dulwich,
london

3. hardlandscaping and
manifestations kingsdale
school, dulwich, london

Detail external elevation: glazed plinth

manifestation

chevron concrete slabs
hardlandscaping

Clear Glazed Plinth and Glazed Link:

Clear frameless glazing forms the glazed
plinth layer and the vertical element
between the coloured façade element and
the Victorian brickwork.
Plinth:
The plinth is formed of clear
double/single glazed panels with
structural silicone pointing to the
vertical joints. Sliding doors are
frameless assemblies with head
mechanism mounted to the internal face
of the glass.
Glazed link:
The transparent vertical element
comprises frameless panels supported on
internal transoms with structural silicon
pointing. The design intension is for a
highly transparent glazed link that
allows for the two buildings to appear
dis-engaged.

Coloured chevron manifestations run
along the plinth level directing visitors
to the entrances and providing Building
Control compliance.

electric sliding door

glass sliding door

interior floor finish

paving slabs
laid to fall

sand bed

Existing floor
slab

4. section detail A-A through sliding
door scale 1:5

while still maintaining the Victorian levels at ground and second floor. Visual autonomy is also created between the Victorian school through the use of the clear glass circulation link. The intention is to strike a balance between creating a strong individual presence for the new extension, while respecting the architectural merit of the neighbours with which it stands shoulder to shoulder.

As of spring 2007, the project is on site, and dRMM are progressing with its detailed design. In keeping with dRMM's methodology, they are working closely with suppliers to devise a novel reconfiguration of the traditional curtain wall system using an off-set cruci-

form grid.

The principle of the façade treatment is to adapt a high-quality curtain wall system embodying characteristics of internal structure, virtually-flush finish and reflectivity, while introducing variation and flexibility to remove the orthogonal grid appearance normally associated with such systems. In contrast to the articulation of its two neighbours, the extension avoids composition. The principle is to adapt a standard system with three types of panels: solid, translucent and clear. These are arranged not by formal methods but by performance requirements of views, ventilation and solar gain. The façades work doubly hard by providing also the internal finish to the classroom walls: the reverse

Planning model: view from Stonhouse Street/main entrance

Planning model: North view

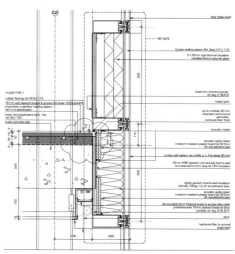

Typical slab section detail

sides of solid panels are lined in pin board, acoustic panelling, and other surfaces depending on class requirements. Windows are manually operated so that occupants can increase natural ventilation.

The façades are bold yet simple, appearing to float above the clear-glazed plinth, and without a separate parapet. The principle of the colouration is to graduate the colours around the building from the existing context: from the red and terracotta of Stonhouse Street, through to the greens of the playground soft landscaping to the rear. The colour is powder coated, applied to the inside surface of the glass and heat treated. The façade specification is relatively expensive for a school, but is considered appropriate in the context of the high quality Victorian buildings it neighbours, and it works hard to achieve both the interior and exterior architecture.

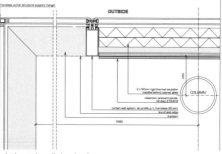

Typical curtain wall plan detail

North Elevation: planning proposal showing colour scheme

East Elevation: planning proposal showing colour scheme

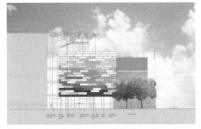

South Elevation: planning proposal showing colour scheme

Colour treatment options developed in conjunction with the school community

dsdha

Client: morelondon
Contractor: Mice Sames
Structural Engineer: Jane Wernick Associates
Services Engineer: Arup

project:
potters' field park kiosks
tower bridge/city hall,
london se1
nearest tube: london bridge

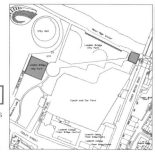

Located in the Pool of London, on the south bank of the Thames, Potters' Fields Park enjoys a backdrop of some of the world's most iconic buildings including the Tower of London, Tower Bridge, Swiss Re building ['The Gherkin'], City Hall – home to the Greater London Authority (GLA) and the mixed-use More London development. Against this backdrop DSDHA have designed two kiosks for the Park, clad in timber, establishing a human scale of architecture next to these heroic structures

The site of the park has previously been occupied by light industry including tanneries and potters' workshops. During the Second World War the warehouses suffered significant bomb damage leading to postwar clearances that created the Park on the edge of the Thames.

In 2004 GrossMax Landscape Architects were appointed to redesign the Park to meet the increasing demands of its one million plus visitors. To complement the new Park DSDHA were appointed in 2005 to design two kiosks to provide amenities for the visitors, residents and local workers.

Blossom Square kiosk sited next to Tower Bridge

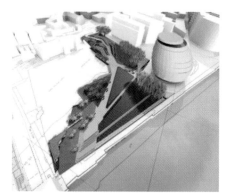

Axonometric view of Parkside kiosk

Working model of Parkside kiosk

View of Parkside kiosk

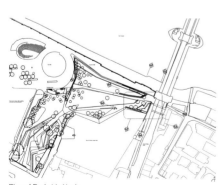

Plan of Parkside kiosk

View of Parkside kiosk cantilever

Parkside kiosk: making of timber sample (from left to right)
"charring", "abrading" and "jet washing" processes

will offer refreshments, sheltered external seating and provide a green roof to complement the Park. Parkside kiosk located behind City Hall will provide refreshments, external seating, public conveniences and storage.

Inspired by 18th century grottos from stately gardens, the two kiosks are designed to act as gateways providing both destinations and route markers for the varied audiences that frequent the park and the adjacent More London estate. The design challenge that presented itself to DSDHA was how to make these comparatively small projects complement and enhance the area's history whilst providing an architecture that could mediate between the competing aesthetics of the monumental surrounding buildings and the organic layout of the Park.

To reflect both the material nature of the Park and the sleek lines of the More London Development, DSDHA have designed buildings clad almost entirely in hand crafted horizontal timber boarding. The sleek lines of each kiosk are then carved away to create grotto-like entries to the buildings' amenities and to capture views into and out of the Park. The remaining facades are clad in curtain walling and timber sheet lining.

Designed as a pair, each kiosk's cladding in Siberian Larch has a different finish to its exterior. Blossom Square Kiosk, so as not to compete with its famous neighbour, Tower Bridge, is finished in a light white preservative. Inversely, Parkside Kiosk has an entirely charred finish. This organic finish reflects both the materials of the Park and makes reference to the bombing that took place during the Second World War.

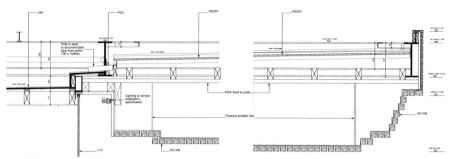

Parkside kiosk: detail through eaves

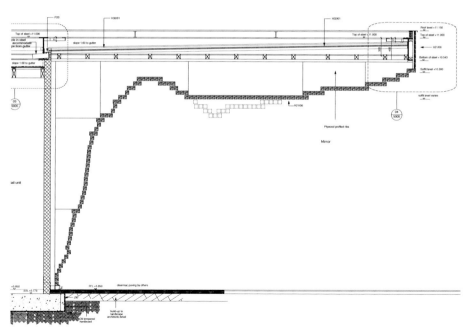

Parkside kiosk: section through cantilever

Blossom Square kiosk: work-in-progress of timber samples

Previously untried in the UK the charring technique is derived from the centuries old Japanese practice of Yakasugi. Through burning wood chippings at the base of vertically positioned boards a charred deposit is created on the surface of the timber. This deposit acts as an effective natural preservative against the external environment. In Japan this method was traditionally used as an inexpensive way of creating a durable preservative to building envelopes.

The charred finish at Parkside Kiosk has been created through repeatedly burning, then jet washing then abrading three sides of the timber. The choice of the relatively hard Siberian Larch ensures that following the removal of charred debris the grain of the wood in pronounced, accentuating the building linearity.

The undulating timber soffits of both kiosks are created through drawing every strata of the building to generate a complete form. Each strata is then hand crafted by a joiner and fixed to a series of plywood 'ribs' suspended from the main structure. Concealed within the soffits are a number of 'canyons' containing artificial lighting and penetrations for daylight.

Each of these bespoke hand-crafted projects have required close collaboration between DSDHA and the joiners to ensure that the completed facades are visually organic to emulate the grottoes from which they are derived, whilst at the same time technically robust to satisfy modern day requirements.

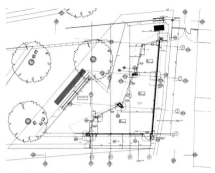

Plan of Blossom Square kiosk

View of Blossom Square kiosk from Tower Bridge

View of Blossom Square kiosk

fat

Client: Sean Griffiths
Contractor: Blake Builders
Structural Engineer: Elliott Wood

project:
house and office
2a garner street, london e2
nearest tube:
bethnal green

The house is situated on a small street running perpendicular to the main thoroughfare, Hackney Road in East London. The area is currently run down but in the process of regeneration. It contains a mix of uses which include private town houses, public housing projects, shops and light industry. The programme for the new building is a two bedroom town house which incorporates an office space, connected into the house, and a separate flat for rent. The design evolved out of an earlier competition entry for a billboard house whose premise was that the front facade would house advertising posters which would help to pay for its construction. The house in Garner Street refines this idea. The front facade consists of a three storey block with three rows of small windows at the top, making it look like a typical, if under scaled, office block. Superimposed on this block is a billboard which takes the shape of a house and extends to form the wall to the garden. The building therefore communicates what it is - a house and an office. The front facade is deliberately 'innocent' in appearance - child like or cartoonish. Its communicative qualities are a reaction against the abstraction of most so-called 'serious' architecture. It is however subjected to a number of distortions which undercut its apparent innocence. These distortions

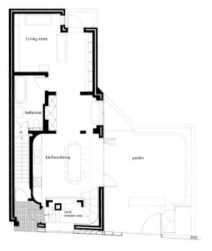

Ground floor plan

View of street elevation

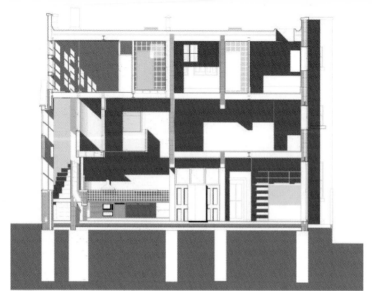

Long section

include its scale, a number of abstract cut outs and additions, which reinforce its sense of being a two dimensional object, and manipulations of window sizes which subtly distort the the facade's sense of unity. The side elevation is another billboard, the sense of which is reinforced by the abstracted decorative cut -outs at the top. In contrast to the front facade, this elevation, which addresses the main thoroughfare, has 'big' scale. The dislocation of scale between the front and side facades creates a sense of tension when the building is seen as whole. It also makes the positions of floors within the building difficult to read which enhances the feeling of distorted scale. The plan of the site forms a L-shape which is closely bounded on three sides. The building sits in the long leg of the

L, perpendicular to Garner Street, leaving the short leg as garden space. This arrangement allows the building to sit snugly in amongst the surrounding buildings. The house is entered through the garden. The ground floor consists of three interconnected spaces - the kitchen which forms the main living space and which opens onto the garden, an intermediate space, and at the rear, the living room. At the heart of the house is the main bathroom. At the front, above the kitchen is a bedroom, which is set back from the front and rear facades forming a stairwell and a light well respectively. From the inside, this room appears to float above the kitchen. From the outside, looking through the external windows, the impression of a building within a building is created. This increases

Cross section

View from street

the sense of layered space suggested by the facade treatment. The kitchen space is characterised by its curved walls and a large fireplace, surmounted by a wooden balustrade carved with heart motifs. This space is flooded with light from the folding sliding doors overlooking the garden, the two storey light well and indirectly, from the window behind the fire place. The garden walls are also curved to create an outdoor room which mirrors the kitchen space. The curved wall of the kitchen continues vertically to form the wall of the bedroom above. The staircase winds around the curved walls of the bedroom/kitchen as it rises through the three storeys of the house. The curvature of the wall gives the staircase the feeling of having been carved out. This sense of depth on the

inside contrasts with the thin, billboard character of the exterior. On ascending the stairs, a half landing is reached, situated behind the fire place. This platform overlooks the street from the lower window of the front facade, and also overlooks the kitchen space from the balcony above the fireplace. This small room, behind the chimney, is fitted with built-in seats including a window seat within the depth of the double facade. The height of this landing prevents direct views into the living spaces from the street, whilst allowing natural light in. From the outside this landing appears like stage, where the movement of people up and down the stairs can be glimpsed. This sense of theatre is reinforced by the 'stage set' quality of the exterior. From this landing the stair continues to

Process of design: Sint Lucas, Holland, showing work on site

wind its way up to the first floor levels. The winding stair reveals itself to the exterior in the doorway in the front facade. This doorway leads to a second stair which runs below the winding stair and which gives separate access to the office space at the rear of the first floor and the flat at the rear of the second floor. The relationship between these staircases gives the building a labyrinthian quality. The first floor landing give access to the bedroom which overlooks both the light well and the stairwell through internal windows, as well as the garden from an external window. Within a nook in the corner of the room is a built-in bed accessed by a set of steps. There is access to a maintenance balcony in the light well and a direct connection to the office from this room, which also is characterised by curved walls. The connection to the office allows for the possibility of extending the office into the bedroom space. The office is L-shaped in plan and provides a self contained working environment within the house. It is characterised by splayed window reveals which maximise the levels of natural light, mitigating against the restriction on the amount of windows allowed in boundary walls. From the first landing the staircase continues to wind around the first floor bedroom eventually reaching the second floor. Behind the curved wall on the second floor

landing is a toilet and shower room. The landing also accesses the main bed room which has two doors, anticipating the possibility that this room could be split into two with the addition of a partition. The sense of scale distortion and theatricality apparent throughout the building is reinforced in this room. The room is lit by the three rows of small 'office' windows visible on the front facade. These windows fragment the view of the city beyond. In contrast to this, another high level window on the side elevation gives a close up view of a section of the rear of the decorative cut outs at the top of this facade. The rear wall of this room is another theatrical set which appears as an element cut out of a nineteenth century house in the manner of a Gordon Matta Clark subtraction. This wall is distorted by the use of different sized architraves together with doors which appear too big for their openings. The colours and flatness of the paint finishes on this element helps to give it an abstract quality when natural light falls across them. These motifs are also evident in other areas of the house. The building is of traditional cavity wall construction and is clad in a fire-proof, wood imitation, cement fibre board, a material which adds to the sense of unreality that the house conveys.

Process of design: Sint Lucas, Holland, showing work on site

introduction
essays
interviews
4 _projects

feilden clegg bradley
architects
project:
london centre for
nanotechnology
gordon street, london wc1
nearest tube: euston

Client: UCL Estates
Contractor: Bluestone
Structural Engineer: Buro Happold
Services Engineer: Buro Happold

The London Centre for Nanotechnology is a joint enterprise between UCL and Imperial College and aims to put British science at the centre of this emerging field. The 8 storey building on a site at 17 – 19 Gordon Street on the UCL campus in Bloomsbury, Central London contains a range of laboratory and office facilities designed to take advantage of the tools which the microelectronics revolution has made available to all branches of the sciences.

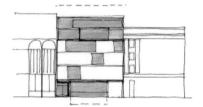

The laboratory spaces, including a 200 square metre Clean Room, have exceptionally rigorous specifications with tightly controlled and stable environmental conditions. Much of the building houses highly sensitive instruments for the preparation and investigation of nanoscale structures and materials.

The fifth floor contains a mix of cellular offices and a large open plan space for research and computational modelling, in a naturally lit glazed rooftop space. On the floors below, additional labs require widely varying internal conditions, from fully air-conditioned 'black box' spaces to day-lit observation rooms.

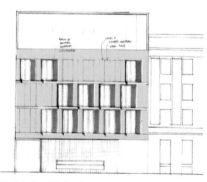

The base is clad in Portland Stone with large glazed openings and white clay bricks facing the courtyard

Sketch studies of the facade

View from street

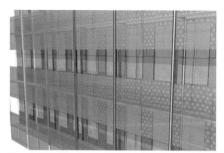

View of external facade

elevation. The central portion consists of a 'layered' façade made up of an inner stainless steel rainscreen clad wall with fixed lights within, steel maintenance walkways between and an outer vertical perforate stainless steel 'brise soleil'. The upper two storeys are glazed full height with vertical solar shading fins.

The building seeks to exploit the material characteristics of the double skin environmental façade to create a 'moiré pattern' - moiré patterns being one of the tools first used by scientists to measure particles at the atomic scale.

The building fabric and services are designed to give laboratories a high degree of protection from elecromagnetic interference, vibration and interruption to electricity supply.

The completed scheme will provide one of the world's leading research facilities in the field of nanotechnology.

View of facade panel

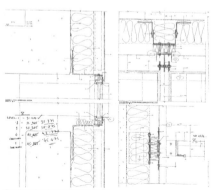

Studies of typical cladding details

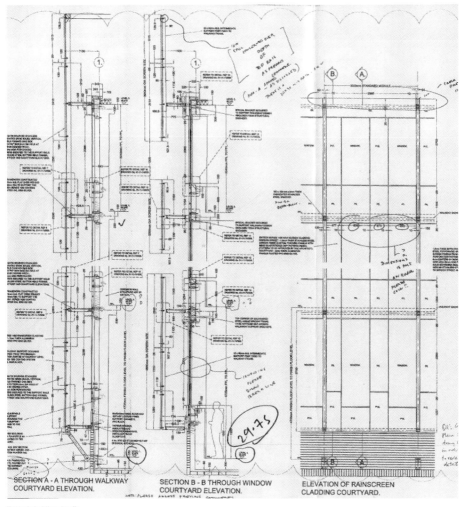

SECTION A - A THROUGH WALKWAY
COURTYARD ELEVATION.

SECTION B - B THROUGH WINDOW
COURTYARD ELEVATION.

ELEVATION OF RAINSCREEN
CLADDING COURTYARD.

Typical cladding details

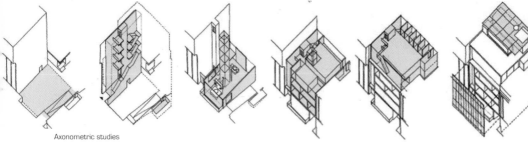

Axonometric studies

Views of facades

Views of facades

Client: Confidential
Contractor: Day Building Ltd
Structural Engineer: Arup
Services Engineer: Arup

gianni botsford ───
architects
project: ───
light house
st john's mews, london w11
(private home: not visible from street)

The project is for the construction of a new 800 m² house on an enclosed back-land site in Notting Hill, London, for a family of two academics and their two children. The clients had previously lived in typical London vertical town houses of up to five stories, and wanted the house to be connected and interactive by being more horizontal. The brief required a very private house for the family to live and work in, a suite of living rooms, a kitchen, two studies, a library, dining room, chapel, five bedrooms and bathrooms, a swimming pool, courtyard gardens, garage, wine cellar, laundry rooms and plant rooms.

As is typical of back land sites, the site had problems of access, overlooking and overshadowing to overcome, as well as a requirement for fourteen different party awards with neighbouring owners. Traditional design processes tend to start with the design, then evaluate their success. This will often lead to inaccurate assumptions and is prone to preconceived thinking. It was realised very early on in the design process that this site was intrinsically linked to the surroundings by daylight, sunlight and view criteria which change throughout the seasons, and these dominated the design approach. The aim was to attempt to avoid falling into 'default' solutions to this design problem through a process of detailed analysis of site and brief prior

View of external wall

Aerial view of roof

View of external walls

to any design phase. Following earlier research work carried out at the Architectural Assocation School of Architecture in London into computationally generated solar form, which is inspired by the morphogenetic processes of nature, computational models were built that, through a 'generate and simulate' cycle, are able to explore the space and optimise potential proposals. The orientation of the site runs almost east-west, and looks towards the more open sides of the site to the south. However, the site is heavily overlooked and overshadowed on the south and west elevations and it was critical to maintain privacy, whilst optimising daylight and sunlight penetration into the house, as cultural opacity in the UK demands sun and daylight to enter the site, to be redistributed, to be contained, and to change perceptions about life in London.

The architects were trying to create an architecture of local adaptation. A general framework was defined that held everything together (not physically; more visually), but that also allowed everything to change depending on the local as well as the global environment. The framework ended up being a 3d grid which itself

View of external walls and roof

became adapted to the local and global environment - the grid spacing, the angle of the roof, and so on.

The architects consider nature to be similar, with the animal body plan which is the same for so many animals, being the 'framework'. Based on this framework, nature can adapt the animal (ie materials and shapes within the framework) to completely different environmental condition.

The environment includes constraints (e.g. design requirements such as daylight levels) and context (e.g. a neighbouring building), and there are local and global versions of both. In addition, the environment also includes what in biology is referred to as 'internal environment' - how one part of the design may affect another part.

The starting point therefore was to represent the empty volume of the site as a three dimensional grid of voxel data points (3d pixels) each consisting of a range of varying attributes. Working with the environmental engineers, Arup, a detailed environmental analysis for each individual voxel on the site was carried out. This analysis produced a database

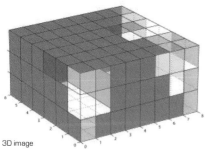

3D image

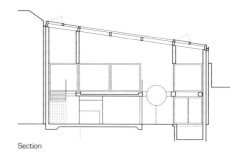

Section

of solar and daylight conditions throughout the year, taking into account weather patterns specific to London. Such environmental data is large and complex and therefore the computer becomes an ideal tool for hypothesising and extrapolating possible proposals. Database mining software tools for the extraction of generalised conditions and conclusions from the environmental data were developed by the architects, as well as a number of visualization tools to understand the data more fully. Some critical discoveries were made during this period which greatly influenced the final form of the house.

Subsequently, the clients preferences and lifestyle were superimposed onto this environmental data. This led to the emergence of a project that was tuned to both the three dimensional environmental conditions and the brief. The section became inverted, placing the bedrooms on the ground floor and the living spaces on the first floor, essentially a double height 'piano nobile'. The inward looking nature of the site in conjunction with the inverted section led to the development of a completely glazed 'sky facade' roof to the house. This 'sky facade', the only visible facade, was seen as an environmental moderator, filtering sunlight and daylight through layers of transparency and opacity. Three different densities of fritting were alo-

cated to the roof panels according to criteria from the rooms below. Solar optimised terraces and gardens created internal courtyard volumes into which the surrounding spaces face.

The empty site was essentially a box 40 m deep by 15m wide, 10 m high on one side and up to 8 metres high on the other sides, consisting of brick party walls. The architects were not able to apply any pressure to the party walls having to build an entirely independent structure, and had a requirement for very large planes of walls extending up to the top of the 10m high wall. In situ exposed concrete was a natural choice - it acts as an environmental moderator (the house is naturally ventilated), the exposed finishes put workmanship on display, and structurally there was a requirement for large vertical cantilevers and beams. A grillage of deep tapering beams span from vertical cantilevers 8m-10m high and 32m long, forming the high level enclosure to the room below. These 'rooms' range in size from 18m x 3m at the largest to 3m x 3m at the smallest.

The roof, although made of 300m2 of glass, has a highly effective solar coating, three different frit densities to the glass, electrically operated blinds, and opening vents, all of which contribute to a high level of control of the internal envionment by the occupants.

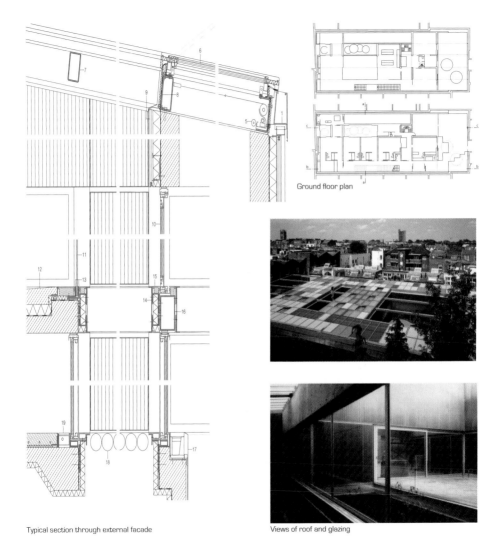

Typical section through external facade

Ground floor plan

Views of roof and glazing

hawkins\brown

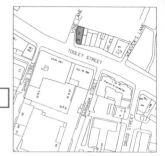

Client: More London Development Ltd
Contractor: Haymills
Structural Engineer: Adams Kara Taylor
Services Consultant : RHB Partnership

project:
offices
155-171 tooley street,
london se1
not yet constructed

The existing terrace of buildings located along Tooley Street is one of the last remaining plots of More London to be developed. Although not listed, the buildings lie within a conservation area and remain a fragment of a former streetscape albeit now in a very different context. The proposal intends to provide a transitional element that joins rather than separates the new More London development with the immediate locality, mediating between the many commercial uses of the estate and the local community.

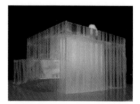

The terrace accommodates retail space at Ground floor with flexible and adaptable space above over three floors, behind retained, refurbished and new facades. St Johns Tavern, the public house on the corner facing the park will be refurbished to accommodate a bar/café/restaurant at ground and first floors, with flexible space above.

Working models for related project showing facade concept

By reconfiguring floor levels and providing a new circulation and service element to the rear, the collection of buildings are considered as a single whole whilst retaining their character as a group of buildings.

Facade

It is proposed that much of the existing terrace is re-

Rendered image from street

View of model

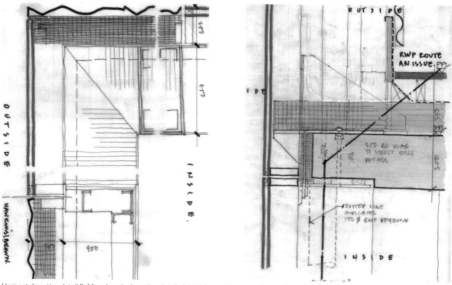

Horizontal section detail (left) and vertical section details (right) from different project to illustrate themes common to the scheme

tained ensuring the best historical fabric is kept . The collection of buildings are considered as one and the treatment of the elevation responds to the entire 360 degree outlook around the site.

The concept of the facade draws inspiration from a parlour trick of lifting a teacup with a balloon. The terrace is analogous with the 'tea cup' as host with the 'balloon' being seen as the new intervention pressing itself against the 'host' existing structure.

The new intervention is notionally visible through the existing elevations contributing to the concept of the building as a host. It is intended that the mixture of the old and new building elements complement each

other and present an engaging presence to the new streetscape. The concept for the new build elements within the scheme have been carefully considered to respond to the new context of the More London estate whilst respecting the existing buildings of the terrace.

The massing of the element draws precedent from the existing terrace buildings. The rhythm of the glazing mullions are generated from the existing window configuration and the massing from the existing adjoining buildings. The rhythm established within the new curtain walling to Tooley Street is repeated around the new build element to the North Elevation. A material change from glass to more solid, anodised aluminium

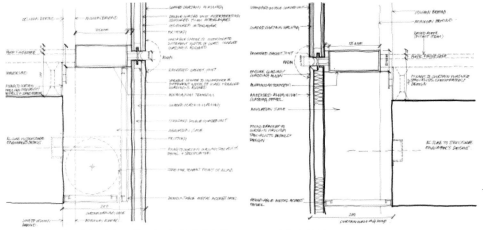

Vertical sections through facade from different project to illustrate themes common to the scheme

panels occurs to identify the change in buildings between 155-169 and 171 St John's Tavern, however the established rhythm is maintained.

The new facade has been designed as a flush glazed system in an irregular pattern with a combination of glass and anodised aluminium panels. The solid, new build element to the rear consists of anodised panels concealing service cores and vertical circulation. The facade becomes more transparent as it wraps around the building with glazing making up the majority of elevations to the South and North, thus maximising the light within flexible workspace.

The glass consists of a combination of clear and coloured glass with varying degrees of transparency achieved through use of fritting and coloured film interlayers. The colour palette was developed by sampling the colours from Tooley Street and the surrounding More London development. The colour is at its most intense to the prominent South Elevation and dissipates as it wraps around the building, in contrast to the solid anodised panels. The use of colour emphasises the playful presence and character of the terrace. At night it is envisaged that the combination of lighting and colour will act as a notable beacon along Tooley Street.

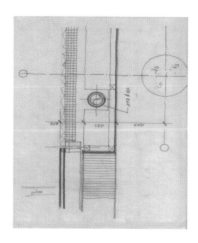

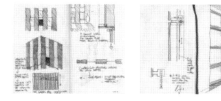

Studies from different projects to illustrate themes common
to the Tooley Street scheme

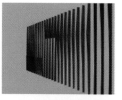
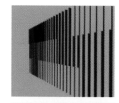
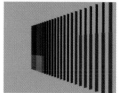
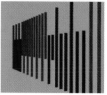

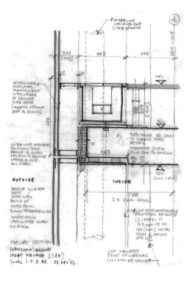

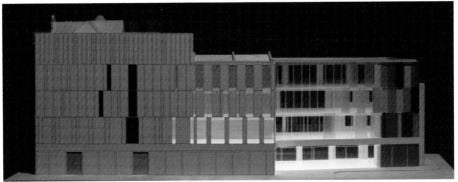

Rear view of model

3D image from street

Client: Tim Fowkes
Contractor: Mark Richardson & Co Ltd
Structural Engineer: Rodrigues Associates

project:
house
103 greenwood road,
london e8
nearest rail: hackney central

Description of the project

A new three storey house sits between two tall 'Georgian', early Victorian terraces in Dalston. It comprises a sunken ground floor sitting within a walled garden that is made of white bricks. Two timber floors are cantilevered over this 'garden wall' below. A sustainable approach has been adopted to the design of the structure and the cladding, and the house is designed to complement its historic context.

Greenwood Road sits within The Graham Road Conservation Area in Hackney. A planning application was made in September 2002, and consent was given in March 2003. Planning restrictions limited the development of the site within the sight lines of the adjoining terrace, and limited clear glazing to the front façade only. A 'family dwelling house' requires >30m2 external space and double bedrooms must be >11m2.

The clients have another house in California and aim to live in this house half the year. He is a carpenter turned developer, whilst she is a folk music journalist. Their children have grown up and left home. The brief was to create a house for entertaining and for it to be made of an exposed oak frame.

Work started on site in March 2004 and the building was occupied in December 2005. The final contract sum was £328,000. The owner worked on site alongside the main contractor, laying the stone floor, building the kitchen & oiling the green oak columns.

The lower ground floor steps in to acknowledge the recessed entrance porch of the adjoining end of terrace. At ground floor there is a kitchen and a glass-roofed dining room that opens onto a dark-blue brick paved garden court. The house façade at ground floor is made of white clay bricks, whilst the garden walls and inner walls are 'Flettons' (red stock bricks) painted white, continuing the material treatment of the interior to form an intimate and private 'outside room'. Disabled access is provided via a ramp that arrives at the glazed dining room door and a bathroom is also provided at ground floor. Two east- facing bedrooms are found at 1st floor. A grand corner balcony opens the tall 2nd floor to a broad view out across back gardens.

Green oak construction

The green oak frame was fabricated by Orlestone Mill in Kent, east England, and erected on site using traditional 'tree nails' rather than steel bolts. Tree Nails

Views of timber cladding

Views from street

Timber frame on site

expand and contract with the column and beam joints, and unlike steel bolts they do not damage the moment connections, which can weaken the structural connection. Throughout, the mortice-and-tenon joints are exposed. In order to satisfy fire regulations, the structure is over-sized to allow for a 'char factor', so that the outer layer of the oak is sacrificial and can burn away without affecting the structural integrity of the columns and beams. A layer of 22mm plywood to the outside of the frame provides structural stiffness. Recesses are top-lit by roof lights and by low-voltage lighting secreted behind oak pelmets. Set out at 600mm centre, the space between columns can be walked into, setting up shadows that blur your peripheral vision, and extending the small spaces phenomenally. In your memory, this tiny house seems to expand also. The generosity of the spaces within the new house, belie the tight site restrictions and the terrace is concluded with this new gesture to the city.

Façade system

The façade on the two upper floors, above the brick base, is made of vertical oak boarding which acts as a rain screen. The oak boarding is supported off the green oak structure via an arrangement of softwood battens. The inner layer of vertical battens holds the

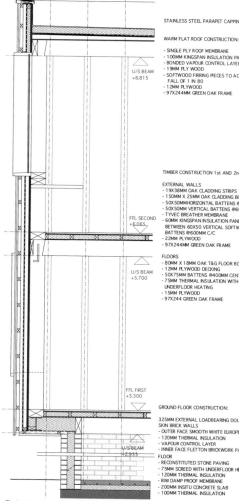

STAINLESS STEEL PARAPET CAPPING

WARM FLAT ROOF CONSTRUCTION:

- SINGLE PLY ROOF MEMBRANE
- 100MM KINGSPAN INSULATION PANEL
- BONDED VAPOUR CONTROL LAYER
- 19MM PLY WOOD
- SOFTWOOD FIRRING PIECES TO ACHIEVE
  FALL OF 1 IN 80
- 12MM PLYWOOD
- 97X244MM GREEN OAK FRAME

U/S BEAM
+8.815

TIMBER CONSTRUCTION 1st AND 2nd FLOOR

EXTERNAL WALLS
- 19X38MM OAK CLADDING STRIPS
- 150MM X 25MM OAK CLADDING BOARDS
- 50X50MMHORIZONTAL BATTENS @400MM C/C
- 50X50MM VERTICAL BATTENS @600MM C/C
- TYVEC BREATHER MEMBRANE
- 60MM KINGSPAN INSULATION PANELS
  BETWEEN 60X50 VERTICAL SOFTWOOD
  BATTENS @600MM C/C
- 22MM PLYWOOD
- 97X244MM GREEN OAK FRAME

FFL SECOND
+6.065

FLOORS
- 80MM X 18MM OAK T&G FLOOR BOARDS
- 12MM PLYWOOD DECKING
- 50X75MM BATTENS @400MM CENTRES
- 75MM THERMAL INSULATION WITH
  UNDERFLOOR HEATING
- 15MM PLYWOOD
- 97X244 GREEN OAK FRAME

U/S BEAM
+5.700

FFL FIRST
+3.300

GROUND FLOOR CONSTRUCTION:

325MM EXTERNAL LOADBEARING DOUBLE
SKIN BRICK WALLS
- OUTER FACE SMOOTH WHITE EUROPEAN BRICK
- 120MM THERMAL INSULATION
- VAPOUR CONTROL LAYER
- INNER FACE FLETTON BRICKWORK PAINTED WHIT

FLOOR
- RECONSTITUTED STONE PAVING
- 75MM SCREED WITH UNDERFLOOR HEATING
- 120MM THERMAL INSULATION
- RIW DAMP PROOF MEMBRANE
- 200MM INSITU CONCRETE SLAB
- 100MM THERMAL INSULATION

U/S BEAM
+2.935

Typical section through external facade

Oak beam

Corner detail

Beam detail

Cladding detail

Front elevation

View of glazed roof

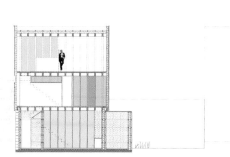
Section BB

View from staircase

View of rear facade

View from second floor

Kingspan insulation panels protected by a breather membrane, followed by a further layer of vertical battens that allow air circulation behind the timber rainscreen, and a final layer of horizontal battens to which the cladding boards are screw fixed. Earlier on during the design phase the architects investigated the use of Kingspan Tekhaus insulated structural panels (SIP), rather than the 'homemade' version of plywood with insulation between battens. The rough OSB finish of the SIP would have required an additional internal finished layer between the columns, which the use of plywood, which was simply painted, avoids. Other considerations of lead-in time and ease of construction on a tight site also informed this decision.

For the cladding boards, kiln dried rather than green oak was used to minimize movement and twisting of the much thinner boards. Two sizes of cladding boards were used. Firstly, a layer of 150x25mm boards fixed with single screws through the centre of the boards with 6mm gaps between boards, allowing shrinking and expansion. The gaps are then covered by 38x19mm oak boards, also fixed by centred screws. Because of the substantial weight of the cladding, extra long stainless steel coach screws were used to tie the cladding battens back to the structure. Stainless

steel fixings do not oxidize and therefore do not react significantly with the oak, which would cause staining.

The architects wanted the building to continue the predominantly vertical character of the neighbouring buildings on Greenwood Road. The elegant statuesque proportions of the rest of the terrace were difficult to replicate on the site as it is wide and shallow rather than deep and narrow like its neighbours, since the site is in fact the garden of a building on Dalston Lane that is perpendicular to Greenwood Road. As a consequence of this rather restricted site and the desire to conclude the terrace and to make it appear influenced by, but discrete from, its neighbours, the architects have loosely imitated the proportions and mouldings of the street fenestration and the vertical striation of the façade helps to make a quite squat little house appear slender and tall. The balcony and windows are framed with projecting oak reveals that mimic the stone window mouldings of the neighbouring terrace. Ventilation to the rooms is provided via hinged oak panels beside the fixed glazing. The southwest corner of the building is lined with translucent white glass panels that are dappled by shadows of trees on sunny afternoons. The oak skin seems to be peeled back from this area to reveal the rhythm the

View of roof light

View of balcony

structure behind.

It was considered to be important to use vertical boards in order to let the small building and the square proportions of its upper facades appear taller and more elegant. The detailing of the cladding also gives the front façade, which does not receive sunlight for most of the day, a more textured, three dimensional quality. This is emphasized when the early morning sun shines on it obliquely. The use of oak boarding gave the opportunity to wrap the building in a continuous skin, rather than create a distinct front and rear as is the case with the existing terrace houses, thereby creating an appropriate end to the terrace.

maccreanorlavington
architects
project:
live-work units
17 old nichol street,
london e2
nearest tube: old street

Client: James Lynch, Beachbay
Contractor: Bigft
Structural Engineer: Techniker
Services Consultant : Freeman Beesley Ltd

The project is located on Old Nichol Street, tucked behind Shoreditch High Street and Bethnal Green Road, facing a playground and the Boundary Estate. This is a quiet area currently undergoing change, characterised by a number of small shops, workshops and warehouses in the process of being converted.

17 Old Nichol Street is an infill site between two warehouses, with number 19 clearly recognisable as a piece of industrial history with its old stock brick, loading doors climbing up the façade and a projecting lifting beam at the top.

17 Old Nichol Street was designed as open plans organised around a stair core and accommodates a live-work unit with a separate entrance on the ground floor and basement, two residential units on first and second floor and a maisonette with roof terrace on third and fourth floor. The rear façade is timber stud, clad in lapped sheets of resin protected timber panels. This is only punched with windows in particular locations allowing for privacy to bedrooms. The front façade consist of large timber framed windows resting on steel channels spanning from party wall to party wall, bringing light into the deep plans of the living room spaces and reflecting a contemporary industrial

Views of glazing

View from street

Window detail

Site progress

atmosphere to the setting. The large timber windows with flush glazing units appear as abstract floating figures along the street and take inspiration from the configuration and the proportion of the façade of 19 Old Nichol Street, making them read as a pair.

The brief for the project has evolved over time. When the client James Lynch obtained the site in the early 1990s, gentrification had not yet got hold of the area but was about to start. Artists had arrived and had turned warehouses into workspace, taking advantage of low rental costs. In this climate, a brief for the building was set that envisaged providing open plan artists studios with large and simple rooms and a "raw" finish, keeping the budget to a low level. These financial constraints formed an approach that used ordinary materials such as blockwork, timber and steel. It was to act like a large shelf with a fully glazed north facing façade.

New opportunities arose when James Lynch purchased the neighbouring 19 Old Nichol Street: The internal layout of number 17 was amended in order for one common staircase to serve both buildings and the pair previously perceived as 'close relatives' were literally combined into one building. Although number

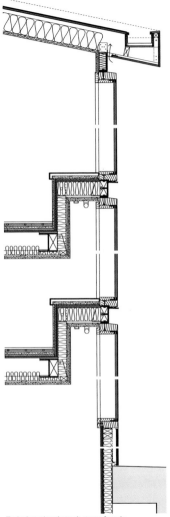
Typical section through street facade

Street elevation

Rear elevation

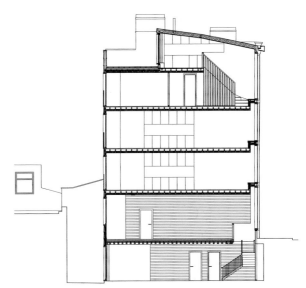

Section

19 was subsequently sold on, the internal lay-out of number 17 remained the same.

In recent years the area has seen a significant increase of property prices and land values. In order to respond to this market change, the brief was adjusted yet again and the interior was redesigned in collaboration with the client: The open plan lay-outs were replaced by two bedroom flats and the level of specification of finishes was generally increased.

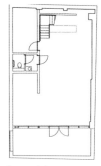

Basement plan

Installation on site

Ground floor plan

1st & 2nd floor plan

3rd floor plan

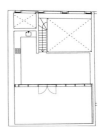
4th floor plan

View from street

View from rear

make

Client: London & Regional
Project management: Tweeds
Structural Engineer: Expedition Engineering
Services Engineer: Blyth & Blyth

project:
55 baker street
55 baker street,
london w1
nearest tube: baker street

This project radically transforms an unremarkable 1950s office building on Baker Street into a striking new urban amenity. In addition to providing increased office accommodation, the development offers an enriched mix of uses and enhances activity and interest at street level by introducing a substantial new public space to the streetscape.

The transformation of the building is dramatically expressed by the three glass 'masks' which span the voids between the existing blocks to create a unified but dynamically modulated new facade. The majority of the existing building is to be retained, with new floorplates bridging the projecting fingers of accommodation to offer a substantially increased area of office accommodation. Full height atria at the heart of these office areas draw natural light deep into the building.

The masks situated at either end of the facade provide double-skinned glazing for the new office floor space, while the central mask encloses a seven-storey atrium, accessed directly from street level and open to the public. This space will introduce a new public focal point to Baker Street as a whole. The ground floor of the building will be entirely re-clad and devoted to retail units, cafes and restaurants. At the rear of the build-

ing, a new development of twenty-three houses offers affordable, key worker and private accommodation.

In addition to the cost and energy savings represented by retaining and refurbishing the existing building, the scheme has been designed to minimise environmental impact and optimise energy efficiency and has achieved a BREEAM rating of 'Excellent'.

Facade concept

The basic concept for the facade design arose from the desire to establish a distinctive presence for the building on Baker Street. The existing structure is a plain and somewhat anonymous building whose length – it is 138m long and occupies approximately 15 per cent of Baker Street's total frontage – means that it cannot be viewed in its entirety face on.

Accordingly, the design team sought to develop a facade concept which would signal the renovation of the building and provide a more expressive and commanding presence in the streetscape.

Rendered aerial image

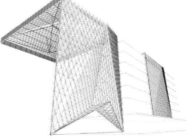
Drawing of masks

Rendered view from street

The concept of an arrangement of folded planes emerged at an early stage in the design process, drawing on the orthogonal character of the existing building but adapting it to create a more dynamic form. The angled arrangement of folded planes allowed the facade to project outwards from the line of the existing structure, enhancing the visibility of the development from a range of vantage points along Baker Street and announcing the radical transformation of the building.

The folding of the roof section of the central mask also serves an important structural purpose. Here, the angled planes offer the most elegant and efficient means of spanning the distance between the existing fingers of accommodation to create the enclosure required for the new development. At street level, the convex folded form of the central mask creates an entrance canopy that draws people into the public space at the heart of the development.

The central mask is 30m high and encloses an atrium which is 22m high and 30m deep. The technical challenges posed by these dimensions required a particularly close collaboration between architects, structural engineers and the subcontractors responsible for the manufacture and assembly of the structural elements. Structural engineers Expedition were involved in the evolution of the design from the earliest stages of the process, while subcontractors Seele, appointed to manufacture the facade structure, worked similarly closely with the design team in order to resolve the design to optimum efficiency and elegance.

Facade structure

Each mask is supported by a steel framework, with that of the central mask weighing 152,000kg in total. The primary structure follows the folds of the mask and is composed of 300 x 400mm kite-section steel members which conceal an integrated guttering system that drains water away to the basement.

The corresponding planes of the mask facade are formed by a diagrid of smaller solid section steelwork, 150 x 50mm in diameter, which supports the glazing. A supplementary system of tensioned steel cables reinforces the roof diagrid.

Concept model

Glass clamp detail

Steelwork in facory (left) and on site (right)

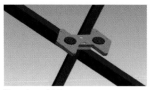

Glass clamp details

Facade structure

The mask roof is supported at its perimeter by the existing building, while the weight of the mask facade is transferred down to the basement by two steel columns set into the walls on either side of the atrium. A major movement joint runs down the centre of the building; in order to allow the central mask to span this the structure is fixed to the existing building on the northern side while the southern side moves on a series Teflon bearings, allowing movement within tolerances +70mm and –25mm.

Glazing system

The faceted facade of the central mask is glazed with a system of overlapping panes of frameless glass, each of which is diamond-shaped and measures approximately 3.3m high and 1.5m across. Inspired by the glazing typically used in nineteenth-century glass houses, this scale effect enhances the play of light across the facade and lends it additional articulation.

Each facet within the facade has identically sized panes, with a slight variation in the panes required for each planar surface. The central mask is clad in 712 panes of glass (344 of which make up the roof, 288 of which make up the facade, and 80 of which make up the entrance canopy), while the masks on either side each feature 316 panes.

For the facade of the central mask, panes are fixed at the junction points of the diagrid, where an aluminium clamp holds four layers of glass with rubber gaskets. The central atrium roof required greater levels of waterproofing, and here the diamond-shaped panes are flush set into the diagrid and sealed with silicone joints. In addition, roof panes are fritted to provide an element of shading to the atrium.

Construction process

As part of the design process, a full-size prototype of a section of the facade and part of the roof of the central mask were built in the Seele workshops to facilitate extensive impact and post-failure testing.

The steelwork was assembled in a series of ladders on the factory floor, before being welded together with interstitial members on site. Prior to on site construction, each facet of the mask structure was test assembled on the factory floor in order to check the geometry. Glass panes are individually clamped on site.

Progress on site

Public art work

Once completed, the central mask facade will serve as a canvas for a vast public artwork designed by lighting specialists Jason Bruges Studio. An array of lights mounted along the edge of the mask are programmed to illuminate the facade with a shifting pattern of coloured light that will enhance the three-dimensional form of the structure and create a striking new focal point on Baker Street.

Image of entrance

introduction
essays
interviews
4 _projects

mangera yvars
architects
project:
residential extension
gellatly road, london sw14
not yet constructed

Client: Worku Lakew
Structural Engineer: Akera Engineers

224 | projects_ mangera yvars architects

The site is a narrow infill space currently occupied by a single story garage in the Brockley Conservation Area, South London. The scheme is slotted between a local shop and an existing Victorian house and is 2.5m wide at its narrowest point. In order to provide as much usable space as possible, the scheme is organized around a structural and service 'island' placed acting as the core for the house. The floor, walls and roof of the house are hung and cantilevered off the island eliminating the need for perimeter structure and freeing valuable internal space. The island also acts as a support for the stair and kitchen. The kitchen is wrapped and twisted around the stair as it rises up making efficient use of the space available for work surfaces.

The house is laid out as a series of distinct 'territories' separated by a stepped 'landscape' and 'mixing zones' rather than by any formal enclosure such as walls or partitions. These territories include the kitchen, gallery, bathroom and bedrooms.

The upper volume is cantilevered and clad in a highly reflective metallic skin. With the absence of any obvious structural support, the upper volume will appear as a 'cloud'-like space floating over the house. The

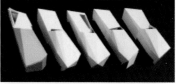

Volumetric studies

Aerial view

View from garden

Views of models

View from street

Mock-up of cladding panels

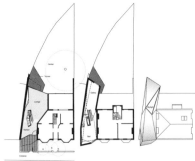

Ground, 1st floor and roof plans

faceted cladding will reflect the sky, providing an indication of weather, season and time, and acting as
a counterpoint to an otherwise harsh inner city environment.

The ground floor lounge is set under a double height
triangular lightwell to roof level, giving the sensation of
height in a small space. The second bedroom upstairs
is bathed in light from a 'light shaft', which projects
to roof level. This light shaft provides a dramatic internal ambience and contributes to the overall sculptural form of the house. The architects are currently
working with a national newspaper to provide a digital
news sheet as the new elevation for the neighbouring
shopfront.

View of interior

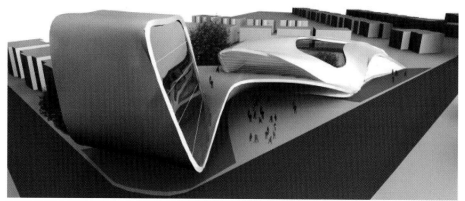

Related project: rendering of Harrow Community Centre

Related Project: Abbey Mills Centre

The International Islamic Centre at Abbey Mills provides a Mosque, School, Islamic Arts and Exhibition Space a Manuscript and Islamic Library, Youth and Play facilities set within a new Islamic Garden. The built area of the scheme will be in excess of 180,000m2 and will be phased over a number of years. The site is 1km in length and sits on the banks of the Channelsea River. The Mosque could be used as the 'Islamic Quarter' for the Olympics and the London Development Agency regard the project as a 'major asset' for 2012 Games.

In fact the site is in the Lower Lea Valley, in close proximity to the London 2012 Olympic sites, which is an area in transition. Newham is one of London's most ethnically diverse Boroughs with a changing demographic profile and growing immigrant community. Half of Newham population is of an ethnic minority origin, a quarter of which is Muslim. The area is key to London's continuing eastward expansion with major regeneration projects underway. What happens in the Lower Lea Valley will profoundly affect the future shape and orientation of London. The heady mix of regeneration, transient urban space, a growing migrant population, and the wider geo-political context in which Islam is perceived provides a dynamic urban backdrop for a scheme which aims to become Europe's largest Mosque and Islamic Centre.

The Abbey Mills Trust aims to create a 'Markaz' or Multifunctional Mosque. A Markaz is an International Centre with a much wider constituency than a traditional Community Mosque. The London Markaz provides prayer areas for men and women, a school, li-

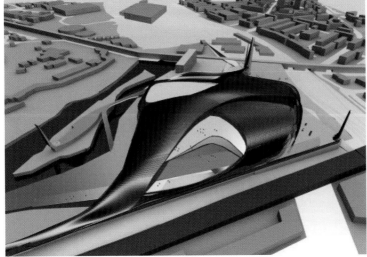

Related project: view of Abbey Mills Centre

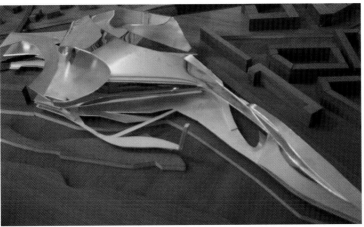

Related project: model of Abbey Mills Centre

Related project: aerial view of Abbey Mills Centre

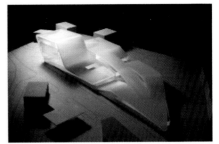
Related project: model of North London Community Centre

brary, offices, residential areas and public space. One of the core principles of the Markaz is to help disadvantaged youth and the Markaz will provide dedicated youth facilities, including sports and recreation areas.

While developing the design, the architects asked themselves 'how can architecture represent faith?' Mangera Yvars consider sacred space to be manifestly symbolic and religious architecture to be heavily weighed by symbolism, often resulting in a parody of itself. The architects also consider symbolism to be pervasive, extending beyond places of worship and into everyday lives, with roadside shrines or souvenirs of St Peter's being synonymous with mainstream religious culture but also commodities which can exploit spiritual vulnerability.

The symbolic repertoire associated with an Islamic architecture may include domes, minarets, calligraphy and geometric motifs. The starting point of the scheme was to question the brief and the assumptions about what an Islamic architecture should be. The question was asked, 'What is a Mosque?' Mangera Yvars considered a mosque to be essentially governed by, and can be reduced to, the etiquette and rules of prayer. This is determined by the Quibla or

direction of prayer to Mecca and lines of the congregation or 'Saf'. The mosque in its simplest form can therefore be seen as a field represented by axis and direction. The scheme is organized as a confluence of Quibla and Saf lines which flow across the site. The project can be seen as urban Islamic Calligraphy.

The scheme interprets the idea of 'Invitation', as a key aspect of Islam, by providing a public space between the inner sanctum of the Mosque and the World outside. The project physically and metaphorically reaches out to provide large urban connections inviting visitors into the building. 'Invitation' space will be used as an outdoor public forum; a place where Muslims and Non Muslims can meet and promote a greater understanding between ideology, faith and humanity.

The structural system is formed by distorting traditional geometric Islamic patterns to form a fractal structural series. A system of overlapping ribs is used with the rib pattern providing a new geometric decorative layer. The structural system is formed by distorting traditional geometric Islamic patterns to form a fractal structural series. A system of overlapping ribs is used which provides a geometric decorative layer which in turn supports the metallic cladding.

Client: Simon Finch
Contractor: RJParry Ltd
Structural Engineer: Ingealtoir
Services Engineer: Michael Popper Associates

meadowcroft griffin
architects
project:
house and gallery
319 portobello road,
london w10
nearest tube: ladbroke grove

The client for this new house and gallery at 319 Portobello Road is a rare book dealer of international repute. His main UK residence is an arts and crafts house in Norfolk where he retreats when not travelling or in London. He acquired the original end of terrace house and shop in 2000 and sought designers through competitive interview from which the architect's appointment followed in 2001. The brief was to provide a London home, a place to work, for entertaining and an art gallery as an extension of his business. It needed to provide a place of quiet and retreat as well as having a presence within the context of Portobello Road market which projected his individual personality and business identity. As the client and family are away for long periods the aim was to develop a series of spaces that could be used flexibly – transforming from house to gallery as required.

Initial investigations concluded that the dilapidated and subsiding condition of the original property would necessitate almost wholesale reconstruction to create sound fabric. The proposal to demolish and rebuild gave the client numerous spatial and economic benefits: the opportunity to optimize the capacity of the site by creating a new basement and to adjust internal floor levels; with the freedom to create of new large

Model showing view from street

Concept image

View from street

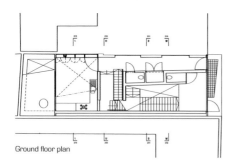

Ground floor plan

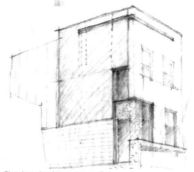

Sketches showing corner studies

open spaces; zero VAT rating of new construction offset the cost.

The planners required that the above ground profile of the original building could not be exceeded and that the integrity and rhythm of fenestration of adjacent buildings should be maintained to the market front-age. The architects were given freedom to change the character of the end of terrace flank wall and rear. The architects concurred that the new building should reinforce the sense of uniformity of the terrace as a backdrop to the 'urban room' of the vibrant market. However, the architects felt strongly that the corner condition should be recognized and the design for a 'wrapped' corner window was accepted through careful dialogue and negotiation. The key horizons of the terrace cornice and shop frontages have been reinterpreted as contemporary elements on the new house façade– high level slot window and slipped floor levels respectively. As a result the street façade is keyed into the proportion and rhythm of the surround-ing buildings. The new basement allowed the design-ers to adjust internal floor levels with greatest height given to the single volume first floor living room. An additional floor has been gained above street level, which, with the basement, has increased the floor

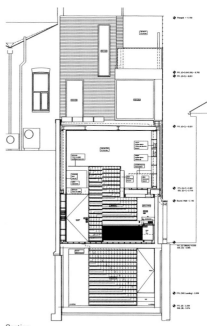

Section

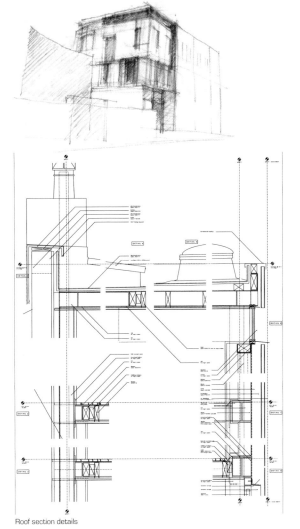

Roof section details

View of roof light

Metal screen

View from garden

Street view by night

area within the original footprint by almost 50%. Spatially, the adjustment to floors in relation to the front windows have created an extraordinary internal pattern of window openings and horizons which offer controlled glimpses of the market, sky and Trellick Tower – a carefully orchestrated 'urban editing' connecting to the outside whilst maintaining privacy.

The building is a hybrid structure of in-situ concrete construction at the lower levels with a steel frame above. The structure 'grows' from the concrete retaining walls of the basement to a point where the steel frame takes over to give unencumbered spans to the first floor room. It is at first floor level that the effect of the new construction is most experienced in this one single, uninterrupted, high, space which is a radical departure from the usual cellular room typology of traditional-build terraced houses. In this space

a 'piano nobile' was created which most directly responds to the clients' range of requirements. At times it can be a domestic living room, at others an entertainment space or an extension to the exhibition gallery. A sequence of double height spaces connects various levels and provides the opportunity for their uses to 'ebb and flow'. The structure reinforces the sense of the building meeting the ground and reaching for the sky which has been a primary theme in revealing landscape qualities within interiors. The most basic concrete finishes were specified with a view to finding virtues in imperfections and to expose 'flaws' which have poetic qualities. Materials have been interpreted thematically to recall the life of the client. Selected areas of raw concrete structure are revealed for their textural qualities which have the character of dry paper and remote landscapes which surround the client's Norfolk home. Stippled concrete

View of corner window

Corner view from street

on the front façade - where city and 'landscape' meet represents the two worlds of the client – his love for the place of his upbringing and his parallel passion for urban life. On the upper levels, relating to the steel frame, materials have been chosen for their qualities of lightness and thinness – perforated metal, timber boards, drylining and glass. Through the use of light, shadow, textured surfaces combined with views of the sky and across neighbouring gardens the architects have sought to create spaces with a strong presence of nature within this dense urban situation.

In terms of budget, programme and procurement, the client was in a position to allow the budget for the project to evolve as the design developed. The client and his representatives were naturally concerned to limit costs but aspired to excellence with best value. The final construction cost was £840,000. Recent valuation of the house was £2.75 million.

The client had no explicit programme constraints. The works were divided into three contracts – groundworks which included demolition, basement excavation and construction including the concrete frame up to first floor level; main superstructure and fitting out. Processing of the planning application took 8 months and through careful negotiation was, in the end, fully supported. Enabling works were carried out during late 2001. Work on site commenced 2002. Completion of 'shell and core' was completed in October 2003 with fit-out continuing in 2003 and early 2004, followed by client occupation in March 2004.

moxon architects

project:
residential extension
25 daleham mews,
london nw3
[private home: not visible from street]

Client: Michelle Green
Contractor: Qube Developments (UK) Ltd
Structural Engineer: Built Engineering
Services Engineer:

The brief was to provide additional space to a much loved mews house to accommodate the client's expanding family. The scheme is in the Belsize Conservation Area of North London and has the complexities of being 'landlocked' between adjacent properties as well as being located above a functioning mechanics garage.

Working with Built Engineers, the minimal and lightweight two storey addition is a combination of solid and transparent elements, wrapped with an untreated Cedar screen at upper level. The addition allows for access to a new full width extension at roof level, providing an additional 5 rooms to the property as well as a largely glazed double height space opening to a roof terrace.

The internal arrangement of the house has been re-modelled, to provide larger rooms with varying degrees of openness in relation to the new elements and a rich variety of smaller spaces for individual or family use.

The envelope is a combination of black rubber and glazing, with Western Red Cedar brise soleil screening both at the upper level. The louvres inhibit solar

Volumetric rendering

View of timber screen

Rendered view from garden

Views of construction on site

gain in summer whilst the lower level glazing and large rooflights open completely to allow for an unhindered stack effect to ventilate the whole house.

The treatment of the new elements creates a modulated façade from outside, where transparent, obscured and opaque elements are suspended above retained brickwork. The goal was to create a distinctive and refined modification that nonetheless retained the compact domestic charm and delight of the mews. On the inside the arrangement allows for far views across North London but simultaneously respects the privacy of the adjoining properties.

Despite significant discouragement from the planning authorities prior to submittal, the scheme received approval within 8 weeks and has more than doubled the usable area of the house, from 61sqm to 132sqm.

The proposal is considered by the architects to be a model for how other similarly scaled properties might be extended and adapted to changing needs – it is manifestly not an extension but a reworking - over two thirds of the volume of the building is new. The reasons for taking this approach in future are twofold: the scheme is of interest in the context of high house prices in the UK and London, and in terms of economics it was desirable for the client to go to the expense of the building work rather than relocate her family. The property is now worth significantly more than its combined initial value and the build cost. In addition, an appreciation for the environmental impact of building works might lead to this approach being more common in future – the efficiency argument for utilising original footprint, foundations and services to nonetheless provide significantly larger living area [for more occupants] is self evident. This can be achieved

Views of construction on site

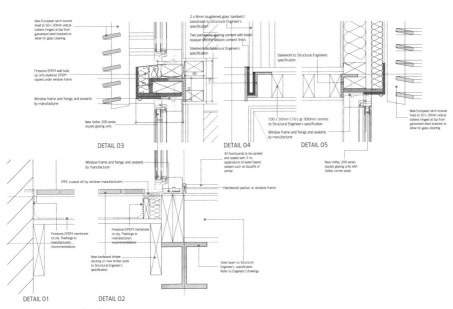

New European larch louvres fixed to 50 x 30mm vetical batters hinged at top from galvanised steel brackets to allow for glass cleaning

2 x 8mm toughened glass 'sandwich' balustrade to Structural Engineer's specification

Two part epoxy glazing cement with black opaque silicone sealant cement finish.

Steelwork to Structural Engineers specification

Steelwork to Structural Engineers specification

Firestone EPDM wall build up onto plywood. EPDM lapped under window frame.

Window frame and fixings and sealants by manufacturer

New Velfac 200 series double glazing units.

100 x 50mm C16's @ 300mm centres to Structural Engineer's specification

Window frame and fixings and sealants by manufacturer

New European larch louvres fixed to 50 x 30mm vetical batters hinged at top from galvanised steel brackets to allow for glass cleaning

DETAIL 03

DETAIL 04

DETAIL 05

All floorboards to be sanded and sealed with 3 no. applications of water based sealant such as Aquafré or similar.

New Velfac 200 series double glazing units with Velfac corner posts.

Window frame and fixings and sealants by manufacturer

PPC coated sill by window manufacturers.

Hardwood packer to window frame

Firestone EPDM membrane on ply. Flashings to manufacturers recommendations.

Firestone EPDM membrane on ply. Flashings to manufacturers recommendations.

New hardwood timber decking on new timber posts to Structural Engineer's specification.

Steel beam to Structural Engineer's specification. Refer to Engineer's drawings

DETAIL 01

DETAIL 02

Section details through facades

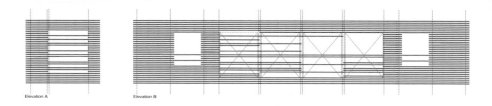

Elevation A

Elevation B

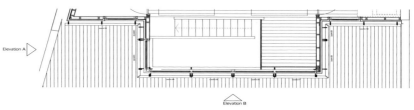

Elevation A ▷

△ Elevation B

Drawing of timber screen

in spite of the seeming incompatibility with Planning Regulations.

One of the fundamental characteristics of this property and similar stock in the area is the relative commonality of approach to the public streetside elevations in contrast to more informal rear aspects. With this in mind the scheme is a contextual response: by combining reclaimed stock London brick with the informal geometry of the timber screen in a fairly loose manner it is appropriately circumstantial and domestic in approach. The façade design is the key component of the scheme – it is the primary element of architectural expression but more importantly the means by which this loose fit in the context is achieved – it is considered as ad hoc in the way it overlaps pre-existing brickwork, new glazing and the black rubber solid elements. The pattern of timber is used to modulate

between the solid and glazed areas, as well as to try and tie the façade together as one unified element.

The construction of the façade is achieved with a slender build up of simple pre finished components. It follows a methodology more typically used on large scale developments with highly technical facades. The logic of discrete weathering layers, insulating layers and solar control / rainscreens as components is more commonly utilised on speculative office developments than it is on residential schemes [of any scale]. This approach was taken on this project to facilitate the type of architectural response described above and also to allow for a lightweight construction and very rapid installation on site.

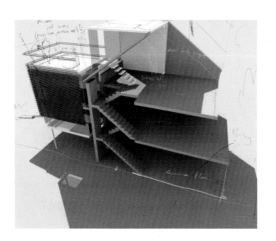

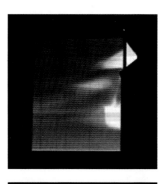

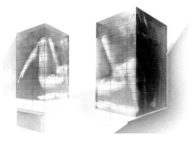

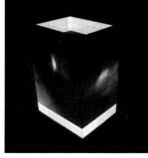

Studies of different perforations of outer screen

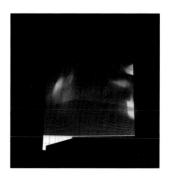

Structural Engineer: Atelier One

muf architecture/art

project:
lowe building
51 whitmore road,
london n1
not yet constructed

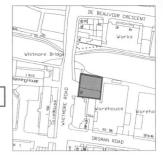

This five storey new build project comprises two storeys of studios and a café with three floors of apartments over and terraces sunk into a planted roof. The first two storeys are a concrete frame with solid timber construction above. The site is at 52 Whitmore Road on the south side of the Regents Canal and therefore opposite the towpath. The canalside elevation is treated as the principle façade. Generally, in this part of London, the south side of the canal is privately owned and inaccessible to the public. In this scheme access (both views in and pedestrian) is made by locating the entrance to the building at the canal edge and cutting a route through at an angle from Whitmore Road framing the water to the street. In turn the selection of façade materials reflects this reorientation to the canal. The canal and street elevations are clad in mathematical tiles. The tiles are glazed on the facades facing the the canal and are matt on those to the street, marking this decision. The architects selected these materials because they are both a repetitive and uniform treatment, and at the same time the handmade tiles, and inconsistencies of the glazes can co-exist in this singular treatment of the envelope.

These brick dimension terracotta tiles, whose use

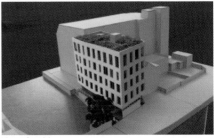

Views of model

East elevation

View from canal

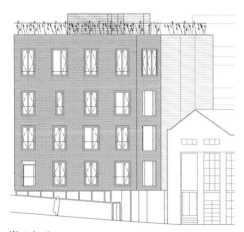

West elevation

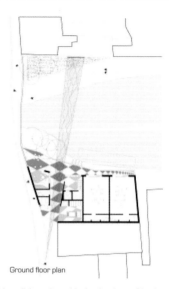

Ground floor plan

dates back to the late 18th Century, formed a 'bridge' between timber weatherboarding and brick in house building.

The centrelines of the windows are regular. The width of the windows however varies from 300mm to 1200mm according to the activities and size of the rooms within. Special perforated tiles then overlay this order.

An interest in revisiting ubiquitous and traditional materials by introducing the hand made and the non uniform at the scale of the facade is a theme found in many of muf's projects.

Earlier examples of this approach to working in this way with materials is in muf's work for a set of 4 metre long ceramic benches for Stoke on Trent. These were

developed in collaboration with the Armitage Shanks factory. Oversized patterns taken from traditional plate patterns were combined with simple forms that accommodated changes in levels across the site.

Simililarly, repetitive GRP panels for façade of the Hypocaust pavilion in St Albans were encrusted with oyster shell and punctured by rosette shaped holes.

Another example is a 7 metre high contemporary folly, which introduces a fourth elevation and completes muf's scheme for Barking Town Square. It is a two storey high structure that is all façade. It is made from reclaimed bricks and architectural salvage on a steel frame. It intentionally refers to the sense of loss, which accompanies regeneration and change.

North elevation

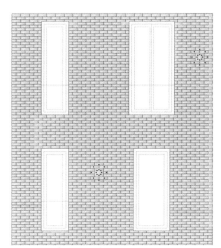

Typical detail of canal elevation

Solid timber panel construction

Mathematical tile

245 | projects_muf architecture/art

View from street

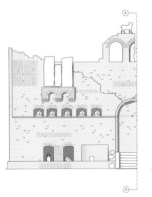

Images from other projects showing a related design process

niall mclaughlin
architects
project:
peabody trust housing
silvertown, london e16
nearest tube:
west silvertown dlr

In December 2002, the architects won a design competition organised by the Peabody Trust. It was called 'Fresh Ideas for Low Cost Housing'. The site was in Silvertown in East London, between Royal Victoria Dock and the River Thames. The architects concentrated on the following design issues:

1. A rational layout of the interior, with a large, flexible living space which has unusually high ceilings for low cost housing.

2. The view from the building, over the strange landscape of the London Docklands: London City Airport, Canary Wharf and the Millennium Dome.

3. The strange chemical history of the site.

4. The nature of modern industrialised construction, in which a timber-frame is wrapped in a decorative outer layer.

Each living unit has two bedrooms and a shared bathroom. The kitchen, dining and living functions are accommodated within a single, large space on the south side of the building. This allows each apartment to make the most of the sun and the view. There is a little south-facing terrace outside each flat, and the ground floor units each have a back garden. Special corner windows on the upper floor flats allow the view to open out along the street towards the Millennium Dome and Canary Wharf in the distance.

Working models

Model of facade

Views from street

Applying and cutting dichroic film to the louvres for the glazed units

Installing the glazed unit

This practice usually looks carefully into the history and topography of a site. Each location has something comparable to DNA, a coded trace pointing towards the future. Everything from local myths to geology can become a starting point for their architecture. Looked at in the context of historical time, this site experienced an extraordinary flowering of industry from the time of the Great Exhibition in 1851 to the collapse of British manufacturing in the late 1970s. In 1850 the place was marshland, by 1990 it had returned to almost total dereliction. The industrial flowering, or chemical-flare, lasted for a very brief period of time. Now the area is being repopulated by a rag-bag of yuppie-houses, airports, an IBIS Hotel and a vast conference centre. It is both somewhere and nowhere.

This kind of place has been called a post-industrial landscape. The architects prefer to think of it in the context of emerging and dissolving landscapes. The uncertainty of its identity is the essence of the place. Its properties are fugitive.

Modern low cost housing construction is pre-fabricated timber frame and timber sheeting. The architects imagined the building being like a row of packing crates stacked up near the water. Once the timber carcass is made, it needs to be wrapped in something. This is usually a layer of brick, or wood, or tiles. The industrial product is returned to a reassuring traditional appearance. The architects looked at kinds of industrial wrapping that might be used as the final

Views of the glazed wall units

layer of the building. Given the site history, they wanted something bright and sweet and chemical. It also had to be inexpensive.

The architects collaborated with light artist Martin Richman for this project; he suggested a material called Radiant Light Film. It is produced by 3M, who make everything from dental adhesive to post-it-notes. It has dichroic properties so it produces iridescence. Colourless metal oxides on the surface of the film disrupt the reflection of light, producing interference patterns that appear as colour. As the angle of incidence changes, the colour changes. The surface, the light source and the viewer are in an ever-changing relationship. The 18th Century physicist and architect Auguste Fresnel discovered this effect and explained the phenomenon of iridescence. It appears naturally in petrol and peacocks wings.

The south façade of the building is wrapped in a cladding of dichroic material held in glass frames. These façade units have a 200mm depth and contain two groups of offset louvres, the first centred within the depth of the case, and the second on the back wall. The louvres are fabricated from sheet acrylic, each covered in the dichroic film. Light hitting the façade is reflected back from different layers, producing a shifting pattern. Cast glass captures the light as it escapes. In time, a stand of silver birch trees will add an extra layer to the façade. They will cast shadows

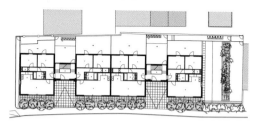

Ground floor plan

onto the surface and catch reflected coloured light. At times the light effect is robustly geometric, at others it is evanescent and fugitive. The architects want the building to have a dream-like quality as though its image will not fix completely in the mind. They hope that this connects to the shifting, uncertain properties of the place.

This was a design & build contract in which the practice partnered with Sandwood Construction who worked successfully with us on the development of the design, as well as the construction of the building. They gave considerable support in solving the many practical difficulties involved in taking materials that are not standard building products and incorporating them into the face of the building.

From the architect's view, a design & build contract allows the architect to havee less control over the detail as the contractor takes the opportunity to detail many aspects of the design. They also see the the the responsibility for site inspections as also changing; the architect's responsibilities are lessened as the contractor takes on this responsibility, with it being usual for the contractor to employ the architect to continue the design development for such projects.

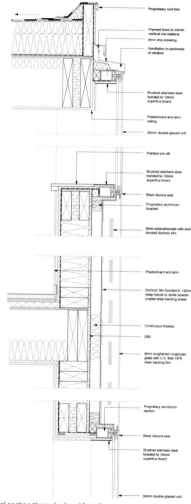

Proprietary roof trim

Flymesh fixed to 25mm
vertical s/w battens

2mm drip pressing

Ventilation to perimeter
of window

Brushed stainless steel
bonded to 10mm
superflux board

Plasterboard and skim
ceiling

30mm double glazed unit

Painted s/w cill

Brushed stainless steel
bonded to 10mm
superflux board

Black silicone seal

Proprietary aluminium
bracket

6mm polycarbonate with surface
bonded dichroic film

Plasterboard and skim

Dichroic film bonded in 120mm
deep bands to white powder
coated steel backing sheet

Continuous firestop

OSB

8mm toughened roughcast
glass with U.V. filter HPR
clear backing film

Proprietary aluminium
section

Black silicone seal

Brushed stainless steel
bonded to 10mm
superflux board

30mm double glazed unit

Typical section through glazed facade

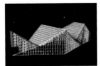

Working models

Sketch by Niall McLaughlin

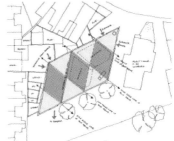

Sketch site plan showing glazed (blue) and solid (grey) roof areas

Dewhurst MacFarlane, glass experts and façade designers, produced a performance specification for the design. It isolated the potential danger of glue fixing the film to the louvres which would become embrittled by UV light. Dewhurst MacFarlane advised that the glass have a UV filter on it to protect the glue, and carried out accelerated testing on the glue to test its performance over 30 years. This process was not fast enough to be complete before work began on site so had to be carried out concurrently. The specification was then changed so that the performance of the façade panels was independent of the performance of the building. By so doing, the performance of the glue would not affect the building's performance. If the glue failed, only the aesthetic appearance of the building would be altered. On this basis, the insurers agreed to provide suitable cover. The glass panels were developed with the sub-contractor. The initial design was sent to different tenderers who each provided their strategy. The preferred sub-contractor developed aluminium cases deep enough to contain the film on offset acrylic louvres. The back of the case is polished aluminium and the front is cast glass with a standard double-glazed seal between. The panels, which act as a rainscreen, are clipped onto the timber frame construction behind. Air can circulate freely behind the panel.

Related project: Scheme for St James's Church, Peckham, showing timber framed structure

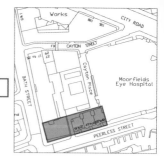

penoyre & prasad

project:
the richard desmond
children's eye centre
moorfields eye hospital,
london ec1
nearest tube: old street

Client: Moorfields Eye Hospital NHS Foundation Trust
Contractor: Balfour Beatty Construction Ltd
Structural Engineer: Price & Myers
Services Engineer: Arup

Client's Brief

Moorfields Eye Hospital is a unique national and international resource for the treatment, research and teaching of ophthalmology. The range of services and volume of patients cannot be matched by any other institution in the world, with over a quarter of a million attendances each year. The Trust's mission in creating the Richard Desmond Children's Eye Centre was to provide the best functioning childrens eye hospital in the world without it looking like a hospital.

The outline business case, approved 2001, stated the new ICEC was to provide the following paediatric accommodation: an A&E department, a primary care clinic for the local area, an outpatient service, a day surgery unit linked directly to the existing operating theatres, a dedicated research space linked to the institute of ophthalmology and a 24-hour short stay hostel patients / parents.

Planning and Social Constraints

The site of the new centre is located within the Moorfields Conservation Area between the existing Moorfields' Eye Hospital buildings on city road and UCL Institute of Ophthalmology Buildings on Bath Street. The local planning authority identified the key planning

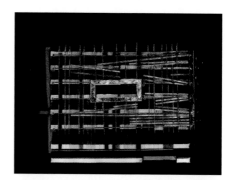

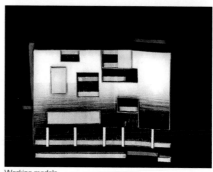

Working models

View by night from street

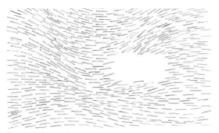 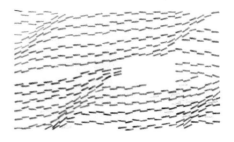

Facade design studies

issues as the height, and mass of the new building and the need for the scheme to be a piece of significant contemporary design.

The constricted nature of the site, the internal layout of clinics and the necessary connections to the existing first floor operating theatres and the research floor of the Institute on the second, all contributed to a clear vertical arrangement of spaces within the eight-storey building.

Externally the mass of the building is lifted clear above a largely glazed entrance platform containing a café, shops and, deeper into the building, the arrival and pre-op areas for the surgical patients and relatives. Bridges cross a slot of space running up the building separating the lifts and stairs, acting as a pause prior to entering the clinical areas and introducing a sense of space and scale. Waiting areas have translucent-coloured play pods, one of which bursts through the floor above, making a table there.

The south façade, facing onto the garden square across Peerless Street, is protected from solar gain by an arrangement of freely placed folded aluminium louvres, held within a large frame enfolding the façade,

on a tensioned cable net suspended in front of glass curtain walling. A projecting bay breaks through the net signalling the most populated part of the building - the main outpatient waiting area on the third floor.

Materials and Method of Construction

The challenge of building adjacent to the existing hospital had the added complexity of functioning operating theatres in close proximity. As the new building could not take support from the existing building a series of mini piles and cantilevered foundations were constructed. The remainder of the building is a reinforced concrete framed building using flat slab construction with exposed circular RC columns all supported on a RC raft foundation.

The main façade is glazed curtain walling with folded aluminium louvres forming a filagree in front. The projecting bay on the third floor is clad in aluminium rain screen coloured bright orange. The east elevation has a ceramic granite finish with circular glazed openings set within it. These 'lenses' give views at various levels internally for both children and adults as they move through the building. The remaining elevations have a calm and restrained appearance, with a palette of brick, render and aluminium-framed windows.

Facade design studies

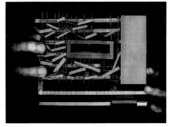

Working model

View from street

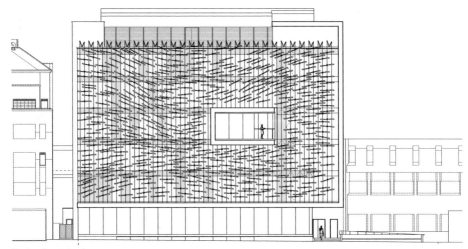

Peerless Street elevation

A design team lead by Penoyre & Prasad was appointed following an invitation and a competitive design / interview process. The project started on the assumption of a two stage tender procurement route. Balfour Beatty were selected on a cost/quality basis from the NHS framework of contractors to take the project to completion.

The design team were re-appointed to the contractor to complete the design. Following approval of the documents in September 2004, construction commenced in October 2004 and completion was reached in December 2006.

Summary of timetable, programme and budget constraints

Competition/competitive interview: November 2002
Design team appointed: May 2003
Planning submission: December 2003
Contractor appointed: March 2004
Enabling works (inc. Demolition):
October 2004-August 2005
Construction started: February 2005
Completion: December 2006

Studies for louvre panel designs

Facade details

Clients: Confidential
Contractor: Bengal Shrachi
Structural Engineers: AKT, Akera Engineers
Services Engineers: NDY, Faber Maunsell

Supercontext

Broadening the spectrum of 'site analysis' - beyond the boundaries of mundane description - and the enjoyment of the uncovered information - beyond a box-ticking exercise in site sensitivity - is the basis of the 'Supercontextualism' approach of Piercy Conner.

In the view of the architects, a Supercontextual site analysis, as opposed to 'garden variety' site description, requires a discernment and subjectivity that differs greatly from passively recording only the most prosaic and indisputable site information. A broader definition of what a site actually is physically, culturally, and economically, prompts focused and necessarily prejudiced investigation into vernacular highlights and habits, uncovering unique characteristics. These broader analyses are filtered for suggestions of potential re-interpretations and re-applications which in turn shape a formal and functional language that is intrinsically tied to the locality.

The architects also consider the most interesting characteristics of a site to lie possibly in 'subjectively illuminated' visual clues, objectively imposed physical constraints or 'witnessed programmatic/ behavioral patterns'. Often the architectural benefit lies in su-

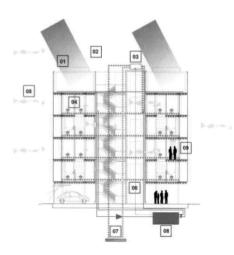

Sectional study

Unfolded facade

View from street

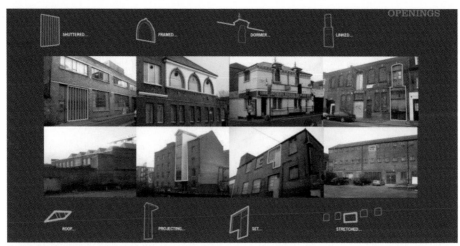

Contextual study: openings

perimposing and cross-referencing various analytical sets of data which at first glance may appear to be unrelated or even contradictory.

Piercy Conner consider that, for some projects, the detailed study of sun paths and their 'opposite reaction' shadow projections creates a template of sun intensity, a template which has facilitated the mapping of areas of density or openness onto the building skin. These studies can be represented as a map of heat and light whereby the transparency of the skin is an inverse of this map – the envelope is directly drawn from existing site conditions. Although this implies a bespoke skin, which indeed it inevitably and willfully is, it is through consideration of how the skin is fabricated that, for Piercy Conner, an economical solution is reached. For example, a panelized system in a limited palette of permutations of apertures and patterns can produce a varied and responsive façade which

maintains its buildability. Furthermore, the parallel layers of investigation direct and coordinate efforts: the grouping of forms to create shared courtyards and play areas benefits solar control by limiting the percentage of façade in full glare during the hottest hours whilst the dappled apertures of the engineered skin generates a rich and decorative aesthetic aligned with the baroque history of the region and create an unfolding narrative of the building measured daily and seasonally, registered internally and externally.

For other Piercy Conner projects, the deconstructivist technique of reading the site as a 'palimpsest' is revisited. As unlikely a candidate as it may seem, a weathered and beaten wall, of no immediate historical or aesthetic value, is considered as the defining site reference on one project. The wall, stained and scarred by years of service with no maintenance is

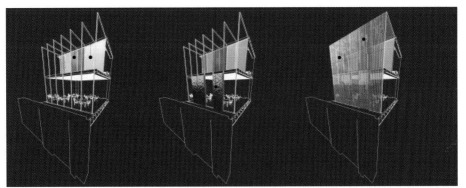

Unitised wall panel   Radiant barrier coated solid panels   Seamless fritted glazing

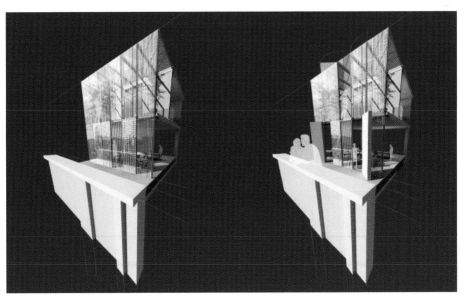

Facade typologies

Contextual study: surfaces

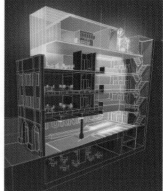

Concept study

read as a quintessential piece of the post-industrial landscape, a document of the changing values and aesthetics of the site. However overlooked and insignificant, the wall may seem on closer inspection to have an unforced beauty that stimulates the proposed architecture. The designed skin seems to emulate the existing wall, borrowing its lived-in elegance. Brick is used as an outer leaf, however: a range of finishes organized into columns of tones and saturations is specified to create a subtly differentiated skin which is site specific whilst utilizing a standard building product. The bands of brick are varied according to aspect – on the north side narrow and erratic in response to the long, oblique views across the canal landscape and on the south side broader and more regular in acknowledgement of the more formal and enclosed views from the street. This aesthetic plays on the nostalgia and romance of faded histories and forms,

celebrating emotional response to the past without resorting to pastiche or cynicism.

Supercontextualism is not intended to produce a patchwork of piecemeal styles and knowing references in the manner of 1980's post modernism nor is its aim retrospective facsimiles. Instead it seeks what is unique and specific about a site, whether dealing with faded industrial landscapes or grand urban monuments, and then exploits that information to create an architecture which has the capacity to resurrect and reincarnate in equal measure. Borrowing and reappropriating materials, motifs, hierarchies, forms and textures from the context allows for place-specific design which is not limited by the site but inspired by it. The subjective and contemporary reimagining and reformulating of the context creates a methodology which is not about constraint but clues and cues.

Contextual study: surfaces

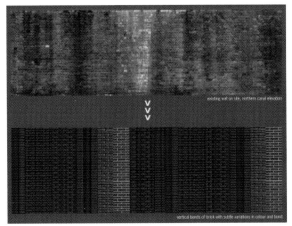

Surfaces: interpretation

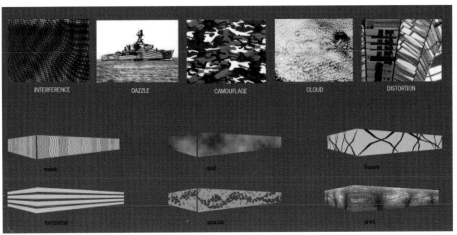

Pattern options

Client: Sarah Wigglesworth and Jeremy Till
Contractor: Koya Construction Limited
Structural Engineer: Price and Myers
Acoustic Consultants: Paul Gillieron Acoustic Design

sarah wigglesworth
architects
project:
house
9 -10 stock orchard street,
london n7
nearest tube: holloway road

The project explores meanings of domesticity and work in the 21st Century. For the architects, the project uses the Surrealist technique of strange conjunctions to challenge assumptions and expectations about the meaning of things. Just as the spaces of the building swap spatial typologies, so the facades swap identities with their 'other'. Moreover it aims to posit a new aesthetic for ecological architecture by the eclectic way it uses different types of materials including farm waste, recycled products as well as both high and low technologies. Materials are selected on the basis of a set of criteria including embodied energy, recyclability, transportation distances, toxicity and so on. Finally, as a self-build project intended to encourage others toward experimentation the architects were keen to use products and materials that could be built using simple, easy-to-learn techniques and in so doing challenge the notion of the 'expert'.

Sandbags

A technique developed in response to the office's proximity to the noise of trains on the main railway line 4m away. Degradable polypropylene bags are the formwork for a weak mixture of sand, lime and cement. Tied up, placed in the wall and watered, the cement mix solidifies and the bag eventually rots.

Progress on site

View from street

View of courtyard

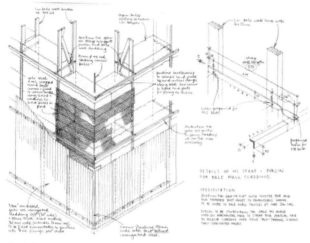

Detail of straw bale construction

View of clothwall

View of sandbag wall

Straw

A waste product from farming, this is both the substance and the surface of the north walls and those surrounding the bedrooms. Nearly 0.5m thick, straw has excellent thermal and acoustic insulation properties. Kept dry and rodent-free it could have a life of 200 years. The architects have detailed it with a rainscreen cladding because the UK climate is so wet. The cladding is quasi industrial, being corrugated galvanised steel. This is normally used in factories but here is used exclusively to clad the house. A small window of the same material made of clear polycarbonate allows the bales to be seen.

Cloth

The cladding to the office signifies domesticity. Consisting of a series of bands of padded rainscreen, it resembles upholstery or quilted clothing. It aims to question our expectations of what offices look like, and it reminds us that our lives are not as compartmentalised as we may think.

Testing, Concept, Research
Sandbags

Research into sandbags led to the Fire & Civil Defence Authority and the Sandbagger Corporation in the USA. The architects discovered the existence of the regulation sized EU sandbag and the possibility of natural or biodegradable alternatives (hessian, hemp, polypropylene) and both porous and non-porous versions. They tested a number of alternatives by filling different bags with a variety of fills and leaving them outside for a month. They decided on a bag that was 200mm wide by 500mm long. Bags were made up to order, in grey since other colours were too expen-

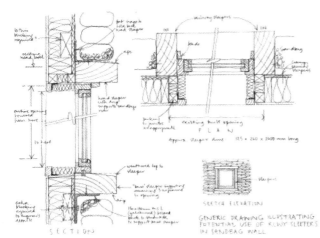

Detail of sandbag wall construction

Laying of sandbag wall

sive. The contractor devised a hopper and funnel to fill the bags with a dry mix of sand, lime and cement. The open end was tied together using an electrical tie. The architects worked together with the contractor to design a system for providing restraint for the bags back to the wall face using a stainless steel wall tie with a vertical dowel. After laying, each bag was bedded down into place using a leadbeating tool and watered with a watering can which began the curing process. Rain did the rest. After a few months the contents had solidified and the bags began to rot due to the action of UV light. The bags have now almost disappeared on their exposed face.

Straw

Most of the information about the detailing of the straw wall derived from two sources: The Straw Bale Handbook by Steen, Steen and Bainbridge (Chelsea Green Publishing, Co. 1994) and a practical course that the architects undertook at the Centre for Alternative Technology in Machynlleth, Wales, where they helped build a new bale structure over one weekend. The designers decided two things very early on: 1. that the bales would not be loadbearing and 2. that they would clad them in a rainscreen cladding allowing for an air gap that could ventilate them should moisture become a problem. Points of detail were that the cladding had to be fire resistant and had to permit the wall to breathe while stopping rodents and insects from getting into the bales. The Building Control Officer wanted an Agrément Certificate – clearly an impossibility - but accepted a lot of written information which was downloaded from the internet. There are many bale-building enthusiasts in the USA that are prepared to share their experience with anyone interested.

View at twilight

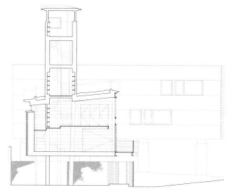
Section

Cloth

The architects wanted a rainscreen with a puckered, upholstered appearance, with buttons at regular intervals. All the suppliers / subcontractors with whom they discussed the facade told them that their wish was impossible, and that the cloth needed to be tensioned. The architects reasoned differently, finding a sail-maker in Littlehampton that made the cloth up into bolts 30m long, in two widths suited to the setting-out of the windows. The outer, visible side is a silicone-impregnated, fire-resistant glass-fibre sheathing. Colours available were white or grey and the architects chose grey. The wadding is 25mm thick quilting and the lining is white polyester. The bolts of cloth were studded with eyelets at 450mm centres ready to be pinned back to the wall battens, also at the same centres. Slots along the long edges of the cloth were designed to hold steel bars to stop the lengths of cloth flapping. In practice this was found to be unnecessary. Windows and copings were provided areas where tailoring was required, some of which was quite complicated. The cloth lengths are designed to be taken down and replaced if desired.

View of tower

View of straw wall

View of fabric wall construction

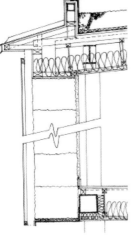

Section through straw bale wall

Orthogonal view

sergison bates
architects
project: ─────
urban housing,
finsbury park, london
seven sisters road,
london n4
nearest tube: manor house

Client: Circle Anglia
Contractor: Hill Partnerships
Structural Engineer: Powell Tolner & Associates

Urban Housing

The project comprises the complete redevelopment
of an urban site on Seven Sisters Road, on the edge of
Finsbury Park in North London and involved the demolition of an existing hotel together with associated out-
buildings and low quality external areas. Seven Sisters
Road is characterised by large Victorian villas which
give the street a distinctive grain. They employ the
familiar architectural devices to support residential
life such as bay windows and entrance porticos whilst
large windows and raised ground floors give a formal
urban scale.

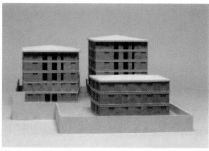

Working model

Three new urban villas are arranged around a shared
space. Each is of varying height and scale, but are connected in their material and form. The two buildings at
the front of the site (Buildings A and B) have a scale
that befits their urban situation and are seen as a pair
(though not identical), continuing the typology of villas
on Seven Sisters Road. The third building at the rear
of the site (Building C) is smaller in its scale, reflecting its 'backland' situation. Buildings A and B are each
organised around a central circulation core, accessed
at ground and lower ground levels and connected
to the outside at each floor via a generous window
opening. A mix of social-rented and shared ownership
tenure apartments are provided within each of the

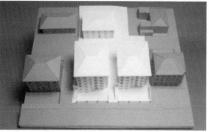

Working model

View of facade

View of facade

Working model

Ground floor plan

View of facade

buildings. Apartments within Building C are all social-rented and are primarily accessed via their own front doors, though a central staircase provides access to two top floor flats. As an instinctive reaction to the architects view of the 'paper-thin expression' of much housing of this type appearing in London and the UK generally, their interest was in developing housing for key workers at low rent or on a shared-ownership basis that felt solid and substantial. The buildings are of a monolithic construction with a strong tectonic expression of brick, render and concrete elements, which represent the structure and give a strong sensation of permanence and weight. With a structure of concrete flat slab and columns, a solid wall construction is achieved by combining a high performance, aerated concrete block with a hard facing brick cladding. The walls are arranged in piers between full height window assemblies and supported by continuous steel angles which are thermally isolated from the structure

behind. These angles also act as lintels at openings and the support provided by these elements at each floor level removes the need for any movement joints in the wall. The brick, burnt-red in colour with flush mortar joints, appears as a monolithic element. This is further emphasised by the deeply recessed window assemblies or balcony spaces behind. The continuous horizontal banding between piers is formed in in-situ concrete and this is returned to create the soffits of balconies and roof. The repeated order of the tectonic facade appears in counterpoint to the gently undulating and modulated external wall. The faint forms of bay windows and set-backs, experienced more explicitly on the 19th-century villas nearby, suggest both familiarity and difference in a way that feels appropriate to the architects within this urban situation. And yet, the space between buildings is charged by the subtle differences arising between building volumes and in their placement in relation to each other.

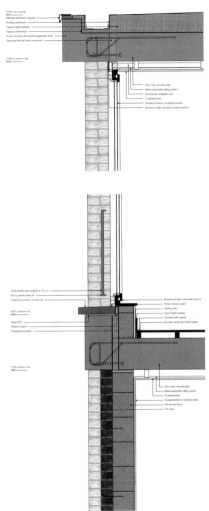

Section through facade

View from street

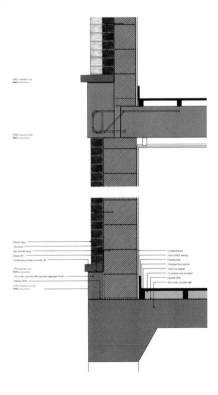

Rear view of Studio House   Front view of Studio House   View of facade

Related Project: Studio House

Located in a previously semi-industrial area of East London which is now dense and fragmented in character, the site occupies a piece of derelict land on a street of light industrial buildings and large pre-war housing blocks.

The complex requirements of the brief with four different programmes; two apartments, a studio for an artist and a space for a joint therapy practice, suggested a form that did not immediately announce its purpose. It can be read as an urban house or a small industrial building and its form is generated, in the most part, by the extraordinary site footprint of 4.5m wide by 20m long and the constraints given by the planning department on massing and sightlines. Internally, the client's wishes suggested a labyrinthine arrangement of interconnected rooms and changes of level much like the spatial qualities of Kettle's Yard, Cambridge and a relaxed definition of the use of rooms which gave a changeable and spontaneous character to the building interior.

Entry to the building from the street is via a porch, open on one side with a mesh screen providing security and semi-privacy. Staircases are placed along one side in long flights and rooms are arranged around a central courtyard which is exposed to the sky. The rear of the building is a single storey with a roof terrace above it at first floor level. The principal space in the top floor apartment is attic-like with a high pitched roof overhead and the bedroom is placed at the front towards the street with a step down where the pitch is at its lowest. From the low strip window in this space views are possible into the leaf canopy of an old Plane tree, the only tree planted on the street.

The timber framed structure allows for the stacking of a variety of spatial volumes within a compact form. The expression of the softwood frame becomes an important element within the architectural language, as vertical Douglas Fir studs become visible within the structural openings of windows and internal rooms

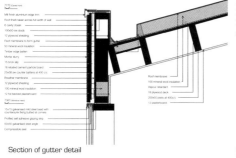

Labels (gutter detail):

7770 (Eaves trim)

Mill finish aluminium edge trim
Roof finish taken across full width of wall
6 cavity closer
100x50 sw studs
12 plywood sheeting
Roof membrane to form gutter
50 mineral wool insulation
Timber edge batten
Mortar slurry
15 brick slip
18 rebated cement particle board
25x38 sw counter battens at 400 c/c
Breather membrane
12 plywood sheeting
100 mineral wool insulation
12 foil backed plasterboard

7080 (Window head)

15x15 galvanised mild steel bead with countersunk fixing butted at corners
Profiled self adhesive glazing strip
50x50 galvanised steel angle
Compressible seal

Roof membrane
100 mineral wool insulation
Vapour retardant
18 plywood deck
200x50 joists at 400 c/c
12 plasterboard

Section of gutter detail

(such as the bathrooms). External claddings and windows are detailed as added layers to the framed structure and become visibly more complex by the misalignment of structure and cladding and the use of semi-reflective glass that cover solid and void alike. Brick was chosen as the primary cladding, a material which is common to the modest architecture of London. However, in this situation it is treated and detailed as a coarse wrapping with a mortar slurry washed over the surface. The construction method adopted on two walls was a brick slip system where thinly cut bricks, bonded to rebated strips are slotted together in the manner of ship-lap boarding to achieve a surface cladding. The contradictory character of the wall, as both monolithic and delicate, gives it a quiet awkwardness and imperfection which connects it with the flawed heroism of nearby industrial buildings. In this way the building adds to the realism of the city condition 'as found'.

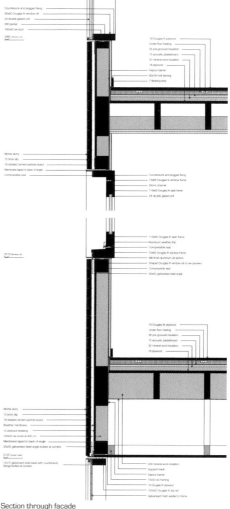

Labels (section through facade):

Countersunk and plugged fixing
65x60 Douglas fir window sill
24 double glazed unit
SW packer
100x50 sw stud

5880 (Window sill)

19 Douglas fir plywood
Under floor heating
35 pre-grooved insulation
15 acoustic plasterboard
30 mineral wool insulation
18 plywood
Vapour barrier
60x18 mdf skirting
7 flanking strip

Mortar slurry
15 brick slip
18 rebated cement particle board
Membrane taped to back of angle
Compressible seal

Countersunk and plugged fixing
73x65 Douglas fir window frame
Storm channel
119x80 Douglas fir sash frame
24 double glazed unit

3715 (Window sill)

119x65 Douglas fir sash frame
Aluminium weather drip
Compressible seal
73x65 Douglas fir window frame
Mill finish aluminium sill section
Shaped Douglas fir window sill on sw packers
Compressible seal
50x50 galvanised steel angle

19 Douglas fir plywood
Under floor heating
35 pre-grooved insulation
15 acoustic plasterboard
30 mineral wool insulation
18 plywood

Mortar slurry
15 brick slip
18 rebated cement particle board
Breather membrane
12 plywood sheeting
100x50 sw studs at 400 c/c
Membrane taped to back of angle
50x50 galvanised steel angle butted at corners

2125 (Cover head)

15x15 galvanised steel bead with countersunk fixings butted at corners

200 mineral wool insulation
Support mesh
Vapour barrier
75x50 sw framing
19 Douglas fir plywood
150x50 Douglas fir top rail
Galvanised mesh welded to frame

Section through facade

stephen taylor
architects

project:
three houses
11-17 chance street,
london e2
nearest tube: old street

Client: Rebecca Collings
Contractor: Charter Construction Plc-
Structural Engineer: Hardman Structural Engineers
Services Engineer: Intengis

Three Small Houses

This project for three houses occupies a small infill site in London's East End neighbourhood of Bethnal Green. Replacing a post war single storey shed, these three storey houses complete an urban block made up of from diverse building types and activities. The brief asked to bring residential use to the site in line with the local authorities' policy of housing growth and the borough's intensification of brownfield urban sites.

Background

The site of this project was, in the eighteenth century, one of the densest and poorest parts of the east end, characterised by workers cottages occupying tightly packed urban neighbourhoods. These cottages defined hard-edged, intimate streets, generally referred to as 'turnings'.

The adjacent Old Nichol Street was once regarded as one of the poorest and crime ridden areas within the East End and appeared on Charles Booth's poverty map of 1889. Of the seven 'income classes' Chance Street and Old Nichol Street were coloured black and represented the lowest class to vicious semicriminal. Damned as 'rookeries', referring to the collective nest

View of facade

View from street

View from street

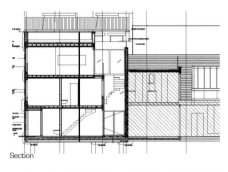
Section

of rooks, the name intended to emphasise the meanness of dwellings and proximity between families. In spite of this they maintained strong communities and were popular with residents.

The subsequent century has seen the urban grain of this part of London eroded, driven first by the Victorian social reformers, then the London County Council, later Greater London Council, and then in the wake of extensive bomb damage of WWII the opportunity to realize Abercrombie's 1943 County of London plan.The ensuing physical transformation to the east end has produce a more fragmented urban fabric with lower densities and a dispersed population, as revealed by comparing the 1901 and 2001 census for Tower Hamlets which shows a decrease in the population of 66% down from 500,000 to under 200,000.

The present day wider context is typical of the physical transformation that has taken place in the East End over the last century where fragments of its eighteenth and nineteenth century past coexist with the myriad of housing experiments that followed from tenement buildings such as the boundary estate to the ever more fragmented developments of the 1950's onwards.

This project for three houses of single room depth is built upon the site of a former print factory constructed after the war, prior to which existed dwellings of the type earlier referred to. Seen as a piece of urban repair this project acknowledges and celebrates the 'patchwork city' in which it belongs its brick façade infills the missing fragment to the urban block of which it is a part.

Cognesent of the 18th Century small London house typology that once occupied the site and the level of urban intensification that came with them, themes of compact urban dwelling are explored through the design of these houses.

Flat fronted and abutting its adjacent neighbours, the nature of these dwellings lies firmly in support of the 'street' and continue to define the hard edge intimate character of Chance Street.

The site measuring twelve by nine metres with a single east facing aspect to Chance Street, is divided into three plots each occupied by a three storey house.

Light and air is brought into the rear of the houses by a series of small white brick courtyards. The inti-

Elevation

View from entrance

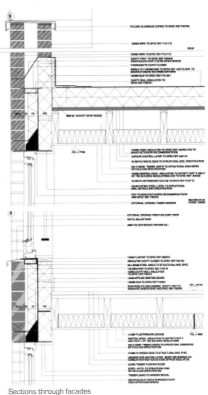

Sections through facades

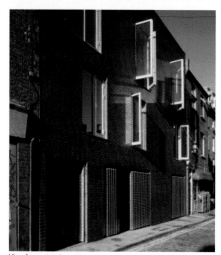

View from street

View from street looking up

macy of these external spaces is both animated and illuminated by the extensive glazed elevations that open on to them. At ground floor, a configuration of folding glazed screens facilitates opening two sides of the courtyard to the interior of the houses, whilst on the first floor the large bi-folding windows that constitute one side of the bedroom open externally across the void of the courtyard consuming this space by its physical action.

The open nature of the elevations at the rear of the houses, with their extensive glazed walls and white clay brick, embraces the courtyards as wholly private spaces. The character and material presence of the courtyard stands in contrasted to the dark brick 'public' façade of the houses to the street, and the part they play within the gritty patchwork of this urban neighbourhood.

Like the generic London Town Houses of the eighteenth and nineteenth century, the configuration of these houses anticipates a shifting of their occupants, use over time, and as such rooms are designed with a view to hosting a range of uses across each level.

Inverting the usual tradition - since this typology offers no ground level garden - dining / kitchen activity is positioned on the top floor, being furthest from the street and benefiting from most light, bedrooms are at first floor and the ground floor considered flexibly for a range uses which may include small work room.

The proximity of such domestic uses at ground floor given the narrowness of the street are given a distancing zone from the pavement edge by large inset porches of perforated and folded bronze 'curtains'.

Views of facades

introduction
essays
interviews
projects ────────

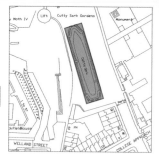

youmeheshe

project: ────────
cutty sark
visitors centre
cutty sark, london se10
nearest tube: cutty sark dlr

Client: Cutty Sark Enterprises
Lead Contractor: Base Structures
Structural Engineer: Winward Dexter
Timber Structure: Cowley Timberworks:

There is no ship anywhere like Cutty Sark. She is the last, beautiful remaining product of the golden age of sailing ships, when Britain was reliant upon the sea and had perfected technology to make some of the most elegant and fastest cargo ships.

Since she has been dry-berthed at Greenwich, 15 million people have paid to look inside the Cutty Sark, and up to seven million people a year pass through the surrounding gardens to see her from the outside.

She is now the only tea clipper still in existence, built in 1869 at the height of British imperial grandeur, named after a character in the Robert Burns poem Tam'O'Shante and designed to win the annual and lucrative race across the globe to bring the first tea of the year.

On the 21st May 2007, one quarter of the way through a remarkable project of conservation and reanimation, she was subject to a devastating fire. A fire so intense that the two remaining decks were completely destroyed and elements of the iron frame left buckled and warped. The Cutty Sark Trust is now appealing for help in order to recover this project.

View of temporary visitors centre

View inside temporary visitors centre

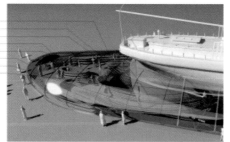

Stairs to dry berth
Retail shelving
Viewing platform
Reception/retail sales desk
Passenger lift to dry berth
Entry/Exit
Ship entrance bridge
w entrance/exit through ship hull

Aerial view of entrance

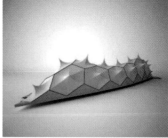

Concept study for temporary museum

The project team will employ the most advanced avail-
ables technology for use on a project of this scale and
importance, without unnecessary innovation. There
are three areas of architectural intervention: the Canopy, the Structure and the Dry Berth.

Canopy

A geometrically and structurally complex glass roof
has been designed using parametric CAD tools to allow a tight fit installation between two very different
existing geometries, the berth and the hull. The ability
of glass panels to be mechanically curved on site allows an affordable solution to the creation of a double
curved surface through use of a greater ratio of flat
panels.

An unobtrusive upgrade to the solar control interlayer
to a higher performing system has been developed to
meet performance criteria set by irradiance mapping
to find hot spots within the accommodation.

Structure

A new structural armature has been developed to relieve the ship of eternal forces. The frame assembly
is a combination of tension and compression members externally; internally tied across the ship beneath
the tween deck (approximately water line if she were

afloat), with diagonal ties picking up loads at the keel.
The system incorporates a replacement steel strake
at the tween deck level, this runs circumferentially
picking up each of the 24 new elements and joining
them with the existing hull. Members, designed to be
interpreted in isolation, form the existing fabric whilst
remaining slender enough not to obscure the visual
connection a visitor needs with the historic vessel.

The Dry Berth

A volume has been developed to provide accommodation that mediates between the brutal form and
materiality of the existing dry berth and the fluid geometry of the ship's hull; this form being key to the
ship's speed. Constructed in engineered timber the
structure provides a flowing surface, capturing the
vortices of forms of water that would have appeared
around the hull when the Cutty Sark was moving at
speed. This assists the interpretation of the ship while
providing all the volume required to operate both the
museum and the events programme critical to the
sustainability of the ship.

An alternative ship entrance is formed; connecting the
entrance and reception area via a bridge to the lower
deck . The components of existing fabric are kept in

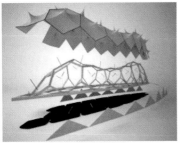

Concept study for temporary museum

Spatial distribution within entrance area

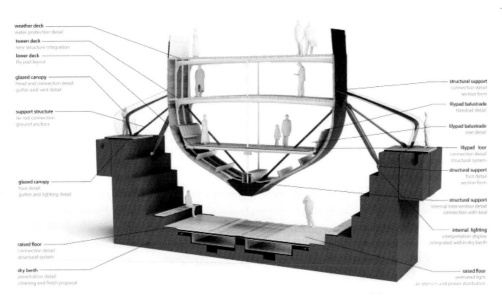

weather deck
water protection detail

tween deck
new structure integration

lower deck
lily pad layout

glazed canopy
head and connection detail
gutter and vent detail

support structure
tie-rod connection
ground anchors

glazed canopy
foot detail
gutter and lighting detail

raised floor
connection detail
structural system

dry berth
penetration detail
cleaning and finish proposal

structural support
connection detail
section form

lilypad balustrade
Handrail detail

lilypad balustrade
seat detail

lilypad floor
connection detail
structural system

structural support
foot detail
section form

structural support
internal intervention detail
connection with keel

internal lighting
interpretation display
integrated within dry berth

raised floor
animated light
air plenum and power distribution

Section through the Cutty Sark and her dry berth

View of entrance

close proximity to the opening, revealing a diagrammatic interpretation of the composite structure.

A simple route minimises vertical travel, whilst providing an intuitive orientation through the dry berth and the ship.

Learning from the ship's history, this grand old vessel has been through several disasters, and survived. She will survive this latest terrible disaster too, and the visionary age of conservation will be rewarded with an exemplary and iconic project.

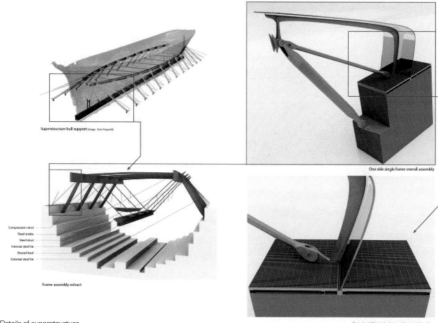

Superstructure hull support

One side single frame overall assembly

Compression strut
Steel strake
Steel strut
Internal steel tie
Boxed keel
External steel tie

Frame assembly extract

Base detail illustrating internal/external interface

Details of superstructure

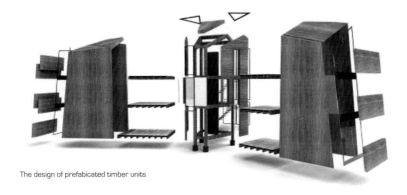

The design of prefabicated timber units

Timber panel types

Related project: the zero energy home
Prefabricated Timber Panels

The timber structure is produced using off -cuts from the production of soft wood plank, using just 2% glue by volume, and although the product gives off formaldehyde (as does timber) the architects are assured that the panels off-gas by the time they are on site. Panels can be constructed up to 14.5m by 4.5m and can be curved; the normal transportable panels are restricted to 4 X 9m or 3 X 11m. Complex abutments can be created, as required where panels come together to form the roof; here the material is cut on a six-axis machine, redeployed from the BMW assembly plant, enabling chamfered edges at varying angles to achieve structural integrity of angular abutments without the requirement of additional support.

Cutting of timber panels

newtecnic practice profile

newtecnic
facade technology+research
www.newtecnic.com

Newtecnic practice internationally as facade designers for architecturally and technically challenging projects and have a particular interest in developing new facade systems and in the use of complex geometries. The company follows principles of rapid prototyping as a method of developing facade systems that can be manufactured quickly and with a high degree of accuracy and precision. Based in London, the office's current work ranges from large scale developments in Moscow, Dubai, Kuwait City and St Petersburg to residential and commercial projects in London, where newtecnic are working with design teams to develop innovative technical solutions and optimise complex designs for digital fabrication.

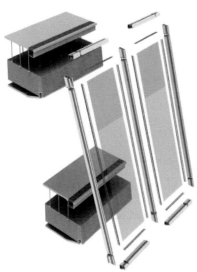

Twisted panel system for Moscow project.
Components in system are modelled for CAD/CAM

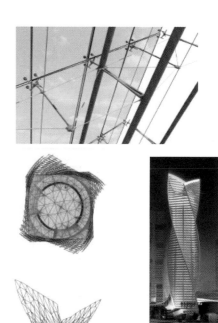

Gridshell roof structure and bolt fixed glazed enclosure to atrium, Moscow.

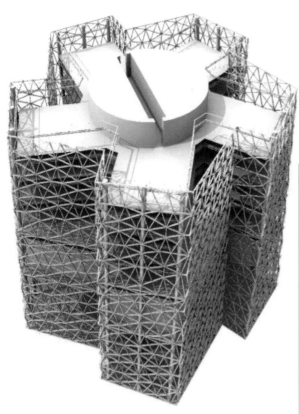

Before establishing their own practice specialising in facades, newtecnic principals Andrew and Yasmin Watts worked extensively both in the UK and abroad. During this time they were involved in a range of significant projects including Federation Square, Melbourne with LAB Architects, the Millennium Bridge, London for Foster and Partners, Euralille and Institut du Monde Arabe, Paris for Ateliers Jean Nouvel, and Cite Internationale, Lyon and the New Caladonia Cultural Centre for Renzo Piano Building Workshop. They have produced a number of volumes on contemporary

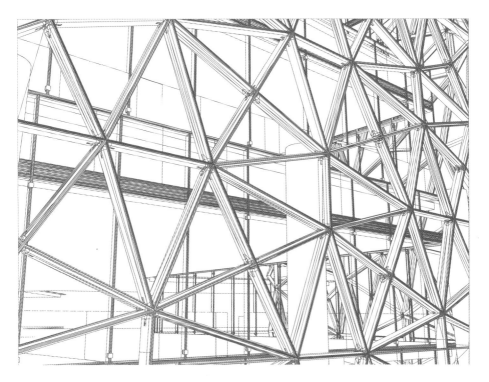

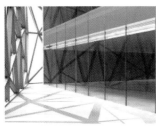

building technology which provide reference material for students and professionals. The *Modern Construction Series* is published by Springer Wien New York. In addition, the *Facades Technical Review*, from RIBA Publications was published in spring 2007.

Andrew runs a postgraduate design studio at the University of Bath which focuses on new forms of construction. He has been a guest speaker at Cambridge University, Vienna Academy of Fine Arts, Technische Universiteit Delft and the Bauhaus University.

Above and following page: Double skin facade system for Gazprom Headquarters, St Petersburg. The outer wall is a series of linked triangular panels that create a crystalline quality to the facades. Panels have articulated node connections that provide a range of panel types from a reduced set of components. The inner glazed wall provides an environmental buffer zone to reduce energy consumption in the building.

The primary structure for the building is set in the interstitial zone between the two glass skins where it also provides structural support to the glazed skins. The facades were developed with a view to limiting the panel types in order to be economic while allowing the outer skin to follow a complex geometry. The project was developed around the principles of rapid prototyping and CAD/CAM.

newtecnic would like to thank all the following people for providing their work and assisting in the making of this book: Alison Brooks & Michael Woodford of Alison Brooks Architects, Lucy Swift of Allford Hall Monaghan Morris, Cany Ash of Ash Sakula Architects, Richard Cottrell, Brian Vermeulen & Bae of Cottrell & Vermeulen, Ciara Devine of dRMM, Deborah Saunt of DSDHA, Sean Griffiths of FAT, Tim Hall of Feilden Clegg Bradley, Gianni Botsford of Gianni Botsford Architects, Roger Hawkins of Hawkins\ Brown, Patrick & Claudia Lynch of Lynch Architects, Prisca Thielmann of MaccreanorLavington Architects, Sharon Nolan of MAKE, Ada Yvars Bravo & Ali Mangera of Mangera Yvars Architects, Caitríona Casey of Meadowcroft Griffin Architects, Ben Addy of Moxon Architects, Liza Fior of MUF Architecture/art, Niall McLaughlin & Kim Borrill of Niall McLaughlin Architects &, Catherine Purves of Penoyre & Prasad, Stuart Piercy of Piercy Conner, Josie Evans of Sarah Wigglesworth Architects, Marina Aldrovandi of Sergison Bates architects, Stephen Taylor of Stephen Taylor Architects, Simon Beames and Simon Dickens of youmeheshe, Scott Cahill, Jeg Dudley, Roly Hudson, Ying Jin, Isabella Percy, Laura Bradley, Ian Darlington, Andrew Scoones & Jackson Hunt of The Building Centre Trust, David Marold of Springer-Verlag/Wien, Will Pryce, Steve Tancock of Latimer Trend, Professor Vaughan Hart of of the University of Bath, Department of Architecture & Civil Engineering.

newtecnic would like to thank all the following people and practices for providing images of their work:

Alison Brooks Architects
All photographs and images courtesy of Alison Brooks Architects

Allford Hall Monaghan Morris
All images courtesy of Allford Hall Monaghan Morris

Ash Sakula Architects
Photographs courtesy of Nick Guttridge, pages 85, 88, 90, 159,160, 161, 163
All other photographs and images courtesy of Ash Sakula Architects

Cottrell & Vermeulen
All photographs and images courtesy of Cottrell & Vermeulen

dRMM
All photographs and images courtesy of de Rijke Marsh Morgan

DSDHA
All photographs and images courtesy of DSDHA

FAT
Photographs courtesy of Adrian Taylor, page 183
Photographs courtesy of Morley von Sternberg, page 185
Photographs courtesy of Frans Barten, pages 186, 187
All other photographs and images courtesy of FAT

Feilden Clegg Bradley Architects
All photographs and images courtesy of Feilden Clegg Bradley Architects

Gianni Botsford Architects
Photographs courtesy of Nick Kane, pages 194 (top), 195, 196, 197 (right), 199 (top)
Photographs courtesy of Stefan Kraus/Polimekanos, pages 194 (bottom), 197 (left), 199 (bottom)
All other photographs and images courtesy of Gianni Botsford Architects

Hawkins\ Brown
All images courtesy of Hawkins\ Brown

Lynch Architects
Photographs courtesy of Sue Barr,
pages 207 (top right & bottom right), 209 (top 3rd from left)
Photographs courtesy of Morley von Sternberg,
pages 209 (bottom right), 210, 211 (left)
All other photographs and images courtesy of Lynch
Architects

MaccreanorLavington Architects
Photographs courtesy of Hélène Binet,
pages 212, 213, 214 (left)
All other photographs and images courtesy of
MaccreanorLavington Architects

MAKE
Photographs and images courtesy of MAKE
Mangera Yvars Architects
All images courtesy of Mangera Yvars Architects

Meadowcroft Griffin Architects
Photographs courtesy of David Grandorge,
pages 231, 234 (right), 235
Photographs courtesy of Philip Meadowcroft,
pages 233, 234(left)
All other photographs and images courtesy of Meadowcroft Griffin Architects

Moxon Architects
All photographs and images courtesy of Moxon Architects

MUF Architecture/art
All photographs and images courtesy of MUF Architec-
ture/art

Niall Mclaughlin Architects
Photographs courtesy of Nick Kane,
pages 125, 126, 127, 249 (top left & top right), 250,
251
All other photographs and images courtesy of Niall

Mclaughlin Architects

Penoyre & Prasad
Photographs courtesy of Lyndon Douglas, page 255
All other photographs and images courtesy of Penoyre &
Prasad

Piercy Conner
All images courtesy of Piercy Conner

Sarah Wigglesworth Architects
Photographs courtesy of Paul Smoothy,
pages 267, 270, 271(top left, bottom right)
All other photographs and images courtesy of Sarah Wigglesworth Architects

Sergison Bates architects
Photographs courtesy of David Grandorge,
pages 272, 273, 274
Photographs courtesy of Ioana Marinescu,
page 276 (left & middle)
All other photographs and images courtesy of Sergison
Bates architects

Stephen Taylor Architects
Photographs courtesy of Ioana Marinescu,
pages 278, 279, 280, 282 (left), 283 (top right)
Photographs courtesy of Simon Lewis,
pages 282 (right), 283 (top left, bottom left, bottom right)
All images courtesy of Stephen Taylor Architects

youmeheshe
All photographs and images courtesy of youmeheshe

Images for the essays are provided courtesy of the authors.
Images for essay by Andrew Watts are provided courtesy
of the University of Bath, Department of Architecture & Civil
Engineering. Office photographs in newtecnic profile are by
Will Pryce.

index